Praise for *Moral Wisdom*

"Keenan's book is sharp, offering constructively critical analyses of fundamental moral theological ideas with a profound respect for the Catholic tradition. Keenan uses his own personal stories to recast moral theological ideas in ways that resonate deeply with our lives. Students and colleagues alike identify well with his struggles with moral issues. The chapters on love, sin, suffering, and mercy are extraordinary."

—Dominic Colonna, Department of Theology, Lewis University

"This is a lovely book! Keenan probes his own experiences of struggle, suffering, and love, interweaving them with biblical reflection and theological analysis. He looks fault and sorrow squarely in the face, yet sustains buoyant notes of hope and commitment. The content of this book is an exercise in the virtue of its title."

—Lisa Sowle Cahill, J. Donald Monan Professor of Theology, Boston College

"James Keenan puts 'flesh and bones' on the abstractions of moral theory and demonstrates from his own personal experience how the Christian moral life is a pilgrimage of faith, hope, and love. Keenan's book will be used widely in college classrooms and seminaries alike. His clarity, honesty, and passion ought to be emulated by every moral theologian."

—Stephen J. Pope, Boston College

"This third edition of Keenan's work demonstrates ever more clearly that it is not a book about moral wisdom but a book of moral wisdom. With an appealing blend of personal stories, Catholic moral theology, and insightful interpretation of human experience, Keenan's volume continues to be a welcome resource for teachers and students."

—Kenneth Himes, OFM, Boston College

Moral Wisdom

Lessons and Texts from the Catholic Tradition

Third Edition

James F. Keenan, S.J.

A SHEED & WARD BOOK
ROWMAN & LITTLEFIELD
Lanham • Boulder • New York • London

Published by Rowman & Littlefield
A wholly owned subsidary of
The Rowman & Littlefield Publishing Group, Inc.
4501 Forbes Boulevard, Suite 200, Lanham, Maryland 20706
https://rowman.com

Unit A, Whitacre Mews, 26-34 Stannary Street, London SE11 4AB,
United Kingdom

British Library Cataloguing in Publication Information Available

Library of Congress Cataloging-in-Publication Data
Names: Keenan, James F., author.
Title: Moral wisdom : lessons and texts from the Catholic tradition / James F. Keenan, S.J.
Description: Third Edition. | Lanham, Maryland : Rowman & Littlefield, 2016. | "A Sheed
    & Ward Book." | Includes bibliographical references and index.
Identifiers: LCCN 2016022281 (print) | LCCN 2016026732 (ebook) | ISBN
    9781442247109 (hardcover : alk. paper) | ISBN 9781442247116 (pbk. : alk. paper) |
    ISBN 9781442247123 (electronic)
Subjects: LCSH: Christian ethics—Catholic authors.
Classification: LCC BJ1249 .K377 2016 (print) | LCC BJ1249 (ebook) | DDC 241/.042—
    dc23
LC record available at https://lccn.loc.gov/2016022281

Printed in the United States of America

To Deb
With Love

Contents

Preface

I was born in Brooklyn in 1953. I was raised there until I was thirteen, when, after the birth of my sister Jeannine, Mom and Dad decided that our family of seven needed another bedroom. We moved out to Smithtown, Long Island.

Growing up in Brooklyn was remarkable. My dad was a police officer, first working in Williamsburg, then in the youth squad, until finally he arrived in Manhattan South Homicide. My mom was a homemaker, and besides raising the five of us, she was also a typist.

Living in Brooklyn, or more specifically, St. Thomas Aquinas Parish on Flatbush and Flatlands Avenues, we eventually became, like everyone else, involved in the parish. Mom was in the Rosary Altar Society, Dad in Holy Name, and I was an altar boy. With my brothers and sisters, we attended the parish grammar school. The girls were taught by the Sisters of Mercy, and the boys by lay teachers in the lower grades and by the Brothers of the Holy Cross in the upper grades. The two schools were packed. There were two classes for each grade in each school, and a class could range anywhere between fifty-five and seventy-five students. I don't know how the teachers did it.

In that environment I learned about the fullness of the church and its traditions. For instance, on All Saints', we traipsed to school dressed like the saint after whom we were named. I had my white robes, white beard, and walking staff; my friend Peter dragged a big set of keys; and my brother Bobby—well, my mom was convinced that the eleventh-century abbot was bald. In that school, we learned about saints, prayers, the commandments, the corporal works of mercy, the sacraments, the life of Jesus, and so on. Each of us had enough theological language at the age of ten that our teachers were proud of us.

In a variety of ways we shared a moral wisdom. What Bobby and I learned in school, or what my parents learned in their associations both in the church and among their friends, was a type of moral wisdom. We—you and I—were taught through a variety of venues and methods to know which values to pursue and which virtues to embody. Sermons and pageants about the pilgrim, the martyr, and the abbot along with their vigilance, courage, and fidelity taught us not only about who we were, but also about who we could become.

That moral wisdom is and always has been available. Our tradition is a lively, life-giving one, even though some use the term *tradition* to halt reflection, discussion, education, insight, wisdom, development, or growth. In its richer meaning, however, tradition is always progressive, developing, and constantly calling us to receive it, enrich it, and humanize it. Entering into that tradition as a community is what I want to do with *Moral Wisdom*.

CHANGES TO THE THIRD EDITION

The third edition has been significantly revised since both the first and the second editions. It responds to more than ten years of the book's continued use in the classroom and the helpful feedback from adopters of each edition. Readers and instructors familiar with the book will find the overall structure and approach similar to the two previous editions, with a couple of significant organizational changes and a number of other updates and revisions throughout to make the book more reader-friendly.

Notable updates include the following:

- Chapter 5, "The Ten Commandments," and chapter 6, "Jesus in the New Testament," have been completely redone and had their order reversed from previous editions. Following the insight of Yiu Sing Lúcás Chan, who claimed that the Ten Commandments and the Eight Beatitudes are the two teaching pillars of the Bible, I now begin the second part with the Ten Commandments, not in the catechism but in the scriptures. The sixth chapter, on Jesus in the New Testament, fundamentally leans on the insight, again brought forward by Lúcás Chan, that the Beatitudes provide a portrait of the very person of Jesus: appropriating the Beatitudes is effectively an *Imitatio Christi*.
- A new chapter 9, "Moral Agency," replaces the previous ninth chapter ("Hope and Leadership"), which was, in a way, simply an appendage. The new concluding chapter addresses being a relational person making moral decisions based on these lessons and texts.

- Throughout the book I endeavor to be more attentive to highlighting the social as well as the personal dimensions of our moral wisdom.
- References and examples have been updated in each chapter.

Acknowledgments

The subject matter of the "lessons" and "texts" was first given as a series of eight lectures at St. Ignatius Loyola Parish, New York City, under the auspices of the pastor, the Reverend Walter Modrys, S.J. Subsequently, I presented the lessons as a series of lectures at the Loyola School of Theology at the Ateneo de Manila in Quezon City, Philippines, under the sponsorship of the president, the Reverend Victor Salonga, S.J., with the kind assistance of Dr. Patria Arañaz. "Hope and Leadership" was a keynote address to a leadership conference chaired by Mr. Francis Butler and sponsored by FADICA (Foundations and Donors Interested in Catholic Activities, Inc.). I am grateful to all these people for making these events engaging, hospitable, and life-enhancing.

I rewrote my lectures while at the Loyola House of Studies in Quezon City. I experienced great consolation there mostly due to the Jesuit community's hospitality and above all the scholastics' extraordinary generosity. Many friends in Manila also made my summer's work easy by their engaging companionship, and I want to name five of them: Luis David, Karen Enriquez, Ritchie Genilo, Yiu Sing Lúcás Chan, and Jordy Orbe.

I want to thank all those at Sheed & Ward, especially my editor, Mr. Jeremy Langford, for their adept and talented work in publishing this project.

Finally, I dedicate this book to my sister Deb. Her life has an integrity, a depth, and a complexity that routinely awakens my rather ordinary life. She touches my life with a grace that has been with me now for many, many years. To her, her husband Gary, and their son Jon, and, of course, Megan, with love and gratitude.

ACKNOWLEDGMENTS FOR THE SECOND EDITION

Ross Miller and then Sarah Stanton at Rowman & Littlefield encouraged me to do a new edition of this book. They canvassed a number of authors and sent me a new set of reviewers' comments that helped me fashion, I think, a better book. I made quite a number of changes. This then is a new edition responding to its last five years of use. I want to thank both Ross and Sarah, as well as the three anonymous reviewers who gave me much to think about and much to do.

ACKNOWLEDGMENTS FOR THE THIRD EDITION

The popularity that *Moral Wisdom* enjoys prompted my editor, Sarah Stanton, to ask me to revisit the manuscript again so as to produce a better book. To help me do so, she chose five faculty members who use the text in their classes. Their insightful reviews have helped me to develop my argument further. The preface outlines these changes in more detail.

I want to thank Sarah Stanton, the five reviewers for their helpful comments, and my research assistant, Connor Murphy. I want to thank, too, all the faculty members who use my book. I appreciate that they and their students find in it the wisdom I attempt to describe.

Finally, while the book is dedicated to my sister Deb, her family expanded recently with the announcement of my nephew Jon's engagement to Sharon Robataille. In their new marriage may they begin together to live as one, as they live out the lessons and texts of our moral wisdom in love.

Introduction

Moral Wisdom Beyond the Moral Manuals

The most significant historical study of moral theology was delivered fifteen years ago at Oxford University through a series of eight lectures given by John Mahoney, S.J. The work was titled *The Making of Moral Theology.*[1] Several years ago Oxford University Press commissioned two American Christian ethicists to bring twenty-five colleagues together to write on different topics relevant to the field of Christian ethics, especially over the past one hundred years.[2] Among the twenty-five essays assigned, five deal with contemporary classics, and Mahoney's book is one of them. In his book, Mahoney argues that the source of the discipline of moral theology is the Irish penitentials of the fifth and sixth centuries. A brief look at these penitentials will help us build a better understanding of the foundation and evolution of moral theology and its application in people's everyday lives.

THE TEXTS OF MORAL THEOLOGY: THE PENITENTIALS, THE CONFESSIONAL MANUALS, AND THE MORAL MANUALS

For many centuries abbots wrote little books of guidelines for administering a fair penance to their spiritual "directees" who sought on occasion forgiveness of their sins. These "penitentials" were later developed from the seventh to the twelfth century by other abbots in other localities throughout Ireland, Britain, and continental Europe. They were, in all likelihood, the only written texts that specifically dealt with morality at that time.[3]

In the early thirteenth century, Pope Innocent III—a fascinating figure who was the first to cast off the title of "Vicar of Peter" in order to assume

1

his newly minted title of "Vicar of Christ" (an enormous shift!)—imposed upon the entire church the Easter duty. For the first time every Christian was required to receive communion once a year at Easter, but in order to do that, they had to confess their sinfulness to a priest. Henry Lea, the great Protestant church historian, called this the most significant piece of legislation in the history of the church.[4]

Since only nuns, monks, and pious noble people had ever confessed their sins before Innocent's edict, this new mandate that all Christians had to develop now the practice of confessing sins demanded that priests be trained as confessors. In 1221, Innocent turned to the newly founded Order of Preachers (the Dominicans) and told them that they were to have as their mission the hearing of confessions. As a result, the Dominicans, an order whose charism was originally to preach the Gospel, were dramatically changed. To meet the papal charge, almost all Dominicans were required to attend daily lectures about confessional practice.[5] The theological formation of the Dominican orders became, for the most part, instruction on hearing confessions. A series of textbooks called "the summaries of confessional manuals," the sequel to the penitentials, appeared from the thirteenth to the sixteenth centuries.

In the sixteenth century, with expansionism into the New World and the Far East, European moralists reexamined what was sin and what was not, especially with regard to the exercises of financial and political power, particularly in lending practices, investments, and maritime insurance issues. In rethinking their moral teachings (always in the key of what was sin and what was not), they speculated a great deal and reorganized the way we think morally. After a century of innovation, moralists settled down and distilled their judgments into textbooks, which were first known as "summaries of cases" and then as "moral manuals." These textbooks lasted until the Second Vatican Council (1962–1965).

Like the "penitentials" and the "confessional manuals," these "moral manuals" were all about sin, and they were only for confessors. They were specifically differentiated from any type of devotional literature that helped lay and religious persons grow in the states of perfection or, as we would say today, into being better disciples.

By the seventeenth century, moral theologians were so convinced that the task of moral theology was *solely* to teach the priest how to determine in confession what was sin (and what was its due penance) that they effectively cut the first principle of the natural law in half. That first principle is simple: avoid evil and do good. Morals were about avoiding evil; devotional literature was about doing the good.

At the beginning of the twentieth century these manuals of moral theology began to appear in the vernacular, though the material that pertained to the sixth commandment remained in Latin so as not to be an occasion of sin for the untrained reader. In order to appreciate just how much the self-understanding of the moral theologian focused singularly on the confessional, we can look at the preface of the first manual of moral theology in English, which was written by an English Jesuit, Thomas Slater (1854–1928):

> [Moral theology] is the product of centuries of labor bestowed by able and holy men on the practical problems of Christian ethics. Here, however, we must ask the reader to bear in mind that the manuals of moral theology are technical works intended to help the confessor and the parish priest in the discharge of their duties. They are as technical as the text-books of the lawyer and the doctor. They are not intended for edification, nor do they hold up a high ideal of Christian perfection for the imitation of the faithful. They deal with what is of obligation under pain of sin; they are books of moral pathology. They are necessary for the Catholic priest to enable him to administer the sacrament of Penance and to fulfill other duties.

Slater noted the "very abundant" literature of devotional theology, but added that "moral theology proposes to itself the much humbler but still necessary task of defining what is right and what wrong in all the practical relations of the Christian life. . . . The first step on the right road of conduct is to avoid evil."[6]

From the fifth century to the Second Vatican Council, almost all moral instruction by moral theologians was to help priests judge about appropriate penances. Thus, when Mahoney claims that the sources of moral theology are in the penitential practices, there is a great deal of evidence and reason for him to make this assertion. However, as we may know almost intuitively, the tradition of moral theology is much richer than sin manuals and strict guidelines.

ARE THE PENITENTIALS, CONFESSIONAL MANUALS, AND MORAL MANUALS ENOUGH?

Many questions arise: Should we look at the history of the moral tradition in such a restrained way? Can we not look at history as more developed, broader, with actually a variety of other resources? Were not Christians formed morally in a variety of different ways, not only by moral theologians and their penitential, confessional, or moral manuals? Were not the moral lives of Christians like Mary Magdalene, Martin of Tours, Gregory the First, Francis and Clare, Dominic, Thomas Aquinas, Catherine of Siena, Ignatius of Loyola, Francis Xavier, Teresa of Avila, Elizabeth of Hungary, Dorothy Day, and others formed by something other than these manuals and their authors? Did their moral wisdom come solely from these books of moral pathology?

If we want to learn the moral wisdom of our tradition, then we cannot look to a history that restrains us. We need to see history as resourceful, and we need to look elsewhere than the textbooks that moralists wrote (though we should not avoid looking at them completely). Indeed, the Second Vatican Council called us to rethink moral theology in its declaration on priestly formation, *Optatam Totius*, when it admonished moral theology that it "should draw more fully on the teaching of Holy Scripture and should throw light upon the exalted vocation of the faithful in Christ."[7]

To appreciate our tradition, I look on history not as a restraint but as a resource and therefore turn to the other four key "texts" of traditional moral formation: the person of Jesus in the New Testament; the two teaching pillars of the Bible, the Ten Commandments and the Beatitudes; the practice of the corporal works of mercy; and the development of the four cardinal virtues. In the history of the moral formation of Christians, these were the texts to which bishops, preachers, teachers, religious orders, lay associations, confraternities, and others regularly appealed in order to become fully moral persons. These texts were the sources for developing our moral wisdom.

Within these texts certain specific lessons have frequently arisen over the centuries that define more specifically the contents of our wisdom. Therefore, before examining the texts our teachers used, I examine the lessons we have learned on love, conscience, sin, and suffering. Why do I suggest these?

My colleague and the Gilbert Stark Professor at Yale University, Margaret Farley, argues that despite all the doubts we encounter in the postmodern world, love and suffering are the two truly human experiences universally shared by people throughout the ages.[8] For Christians, I would add that the experiences of conscience and sin are two other certain realities of our lives. Together these four experiences and the lessons they teach are the most important in the history of Christian moral wisdom. This book is an invitation to explore these experiences and lessons more fully and to apply them to our daily lives.

I believe, then, that by reflecting on each of these texts and lessons, you and I can get into contact once again with the formative influences of the heritage we share. We can come once again to appreciate and understand what gives meaning to our lives and what enhances our relationships with friends and family. As we finish these chapters, realizing that by looking back we can better understand where we are, I turn to the concluding chapter to look ahead. There I conclude by looking at how we can apply our lessons and texts so as to make moral decisions that advance the ways we may become better disciples of Jesus.

Part I

The Lessons

Chapter One

Love

ORDINARY STORIES

I think a lot of the people whom I love. I think especially of my younger brother Bobby. He was born 360 days after I was. My parents always told me that he was my first birthday present. In our childhood, we got along rather well. As a child, I loved Bobby. But I was an odd child. Until I was four years old, I never talked in anything but gibberish. The pediatrician kept insisting that in due time I'd figure out a right way of talking. In the meantime, Bobby was my translator.

"Do you two want to go out?" my mom would ask. I would answer in my own way, but my mom and dad had no idea what I was saying. After I finished saying everything that I thought was important, my mom would turn to Bobby, who would tell her what he wanted and what I meant to say.

We grew up in Brooklyn. My dad was a cop with two side jobs: delivering newspapers and baked goods. My mom was busy raising five children, and having been trained as a secretary, she did a lot of contracted typing at home.

We were an ambitious working-class family with a tight regimen. My parents examined us every night on our homework, were active in several parish organizations, and still had time for TV and family events.

I remember my brother Bobby especially because every year come February, we had three birthdays in a row: my dad's on February 3, Bobby's on February 10, mine on February 15. During the second week of February, my parents would invite about a dozen of our friends to a rather creative birthday party. My folks always had a different party theme: circus clowns, pirates, farmers, and so on. These were imaginative events, complete with costuming, a great deal of care, and a lot of aluminum foil (amazing what the working class can do with aluminum foil to jazz up an event).

The party would be between the tenth and the fifteenth of February, when Bobby and I were literally the same age. These birthday parties continued into our early adolescence. They were more exciting than Christmas. It was not my birthday—I never celebrated a birthday alone—it was Bobby's and mine. And it was not on his birthday or mine, but in between, because it was ours. And Bobby and I were happy with that because we were best friends.

Bobby died at twenty-six. Since then, nothing makes me more conflicted than *my* birthday. The happiest day was when we celebrated together, but now I miss him. I feel very incomplete in losing him. We were very much a pair.

My brother's death shattered us all. I won't dwell on that, but rather on the many lessons we subsequently learned from his death. One was the importance of declaring our love for one another. My dad and mom wondered whether we told one another clearly enough that we love each other. So they began the practice of concluding their phone conversations with us by saying, "I love you."

We have been doing that for the nearly forty years since his death. Every phone call concludes with those words, not only those calls with my mom, but with my cousin Michael, my sisters, and my brother, and now with my nephews and nieces. We do not say "good-bye." We say "I love you."

These are, of course, the same words that we heard of on September 11, 2001. On September 11 we were exposed to the first extraordinary accounts of the major concerns that people wanted to express when they suddenly, without any preparation, faced immediate, unexpected death.

Aristotle taught us that the unexpected reveals the true person. Without the opportunity to think ahead, a surprise catches us off guard and our true instincts emerge. On September 11, we learned what is really important. In all those truly awful cell phone conversations from passengers on the planes that became weapons and from inside the buildings that became morgues, we heard repeatedly the words "I love you," "Tell the children of my love." One extraordinary account after another told the same words. There was not any other comparable expression or interest conveyed. There were no records of people calling to express anger, hate, or resentment. As many incredibly healthy and successful people faced unexpected, imminent death, they almost all tried to do the same thing: they wanted to contact another, someone important to them, and express in their dying words, "I love you."

They did not ask, "Do you love me?" As they faced death and separation, as they were filled with panic imagining how they could ever escape from each of the 110 stories of the buildings, their frightened spirits paused for a moment and rolled out of themselves to another to say "I love you." The human spirit is extraordinary in moving beyond itself. The human spirit so clearly feels how incomplete it is that it moves relentlessly toward union with others.

UNION

I love the word *union*. That is what I felt with Bobby. It is also what those people on September 11 were reaching out for as they faced death.

Thomas Aquinas used *union* to talk about charity. By charity, he said, we are in union with God, neighbor, and self (*Summa Theologiae* II.II.23). Union is what we feel when we love. It is what a couple feels, a sibling, a child, a parent, a friend feels; that union is the desire to deepen union with another. As the twin towers were about to fall, love—the search for union—was a more apparent concern than hatred for those who did this, than fear of what was about to happen. In the last minutes of their lives, love and union is what they wanted to experience.

My friend Doris Donnelly, the director of the Cardinal Suenens Center at John Carroll University, tells the story of a young woman on the flight that crashed into the Pentagon. When the passengers realized there was a problem onboard, many began using their cell phones and learned that the towers had been attacked by other planes. These terrified passengers understood that a similar fate awaited them. After making a call with her cell phone, an older woman offered it to the younger woman seated next to her. The younger woman called her mother. The mother stayed on the phone, telling her daughter that she would stay with her all the way, that she wanted her to see that she was holding her as she held her when she was a baby. She wanted her daughter not to be alone. She wanted her to know of the consolation of union. The mother, too, had the presence of mind to recognize the generosity and concern of the elderly woman; she wanted her daughter to know that the woman next to her cared for her and that she should care for the woman. In an extraordinary moment, not unlike that of Jesus's crucifixion when Jesus spoke respectively to his mother, Mary, and his beloved disciple John, "Mother, behold your son; Son, behold your mother" (John 19:26–27), this woman was telling her daughter that she should see the older woman as her mother and that the older woman should see the young woman as her daughter. She stayed in union with the two of them until their deaths.

I tell these stories because when theologians start talking about love, it often loses its visceral sense. If we take the visceral meaning out of love, we sap it of its energy. We need to feel that sense of union. Union has a very deeply felt, passionate, emotionally invested, human meaning. Union is what we all seek.

About twelve years ago, my dad had a coronary crisis and needed emergency bypass surgery. The operation was somewhat successful, but only two months later my parents' beautiful home on Long Island's north shore was destroyed in a fire. For the subsequent seven months, my parents lived in a motel as they had contractors rebuild their home, aiming to sell it and retire to Florida.

From Fordham University in the Bronx, where I was teaching, I would drive out to Long Island several times a week to have dinner with them. It was always good. I wanted to be with them. Sometimes, though, my dad would be pushing it a little too hard. "Dad, slow down," I would say. "I just want to get out of this motel and down to Florida and sit on the beach holding your mother's hand." (Sadly, it never happened; Dad died of a heart attack shortly after they moved to Florida.)

The call to union, the experience that we have of wanting to be together, is really extraordinary. It is deeply instinctive and existential. So let me conclude this section, on a lighter note, with another story about holding hands.

In 1982 I moved to Rome to do doctoral study for five years. I flew on a very cheap flight. I was sitting next to the window, and the people next to me were a married couple. He had been wounded in Sicily during World War II and left to die in a barn. Days later some people found him unconscious, near death. Now forty years later, he was flying with his wife to find the barn. He wanted to revisit this place. Her name was Marcella Clarke and she asked about me, and I remarked that I was a Jesuit. She responded that her cousin was a Jesuit from my province and his name was Tom Clarke. I told her that I knew him well, that I had just had dinner with him, and that he had an uncle who owned P.J. Clarke's, a famous New York saloon and my parents' favorite bar there. "My father's place!" said Marcella.

After seeing how familiar our worlds were, we hit turbulence. Not your regular turbulence, mind you—we were riding a roller coaster. We were bouncing all over the place. We were deathly afraid and the turbulence lasted several hours. What did we do? Marcella, seated between her husband and me, grabbed our hands. She was not doing it to comfort me and him, nor to be consoled by us. She simply realized that we needed to be holding on to one another. Soon I realized everyone around us was holding hands. Why? If the plane broke in two, would it keep us from being any less shattered? Would holding hands break the impact of our falling to our deaths? Rather than holding onto dear life by holding onto our seats, we wanted to hold on to one another.

STARTING WITH LOVE

I teach an introductory course on moral theology, and during my twenty-nine years teaching it, I only recently learned to begin my course on the topic of love. Until then, not only did I not begin with love, I never even taught a class on it.

For me, love was what the philosophers call "formal." God loves us; we love God; we are called to morality as a response to that love, so let's discuss morality. There was nothing on the experience of love or union—nothing felt, nothing spiritual. It was a principle. Love God. How do I love God? Follow God's law. Admittedly, like all Christians I acknowledged that love has always been the foundation of my life and, in particular, my ethical vision. I also recognized that love was charity and nothing more or less. But I took it all for granted.

I began my course on freedom, a freedom for God, church, and neighbor. I was basically following my mentor, Josef Fuchs, who said that the beginning of all morality depends on personal freedom or basic freedom, a freedom in grace to realize the call of Christ.[1] Many other moral theologians from Europe started the same way. They did this because of their own experience in World War II. With such oppressive movements like the Nazis in Germany and the Fascists in Italy and Spain, moral theologians realized that freedom was the foundation for being moral. No freedom, no ability to pursue the good. Moreover, they did not understand freedom as a freedom to do whatever one wanted to do. Rather, freedom was what we needed to follow Christ. Without the grace of freedom, we could not pick up our cross and follow him.

Pope John Paul II and Cardinal Joseph Ratzinger usually began their writings on morality with truth.[2] They talked about the need to base all ethics on truth. In many ways the tension between moral theologians and teachers of the moral magisterium has been the preference each side has for either freedom or truth. One is looking more at the person, the other more at moral objectivity.

When Cardinal Ratzinger became Pope Benedict XVI, however, he made it clear that he wanted his teachings to start on love. He promulgated his encyclical *Deus Caritas Est* (*God Is Love*) on December 25, 2005, the first Christmas of his pontificate. In the opening paragraph, he summarizes his interest in making an encyclical on love his first one.

> In a world where the name of God is sometimes associated with vengeance or even a duty of hatred and violence, this message is both timely and significant. For this reason, I wish in my first Encyclical to speak of the love which God lavishes upon us and which we in turn must share with others.[3]

Like the pope, I believe we need to start with the primacy of love and specifically the love of God. Why love?

If we start with love instead of freedom or truth, what happens? Why start discussions of morality and ethics with love? Let me give you three rea-

sons—from the scriptures, theology, and the tradition rooted in human experience—for starting with the love of God.

First, the scriptures command it. Jesus teaches us that the two great commandments are to love God and the neighbor as oneself (Mark 12:30–31). Of
course, Jesus is summing up the entire teaching of the law and the prophets.
So, for instance, the Ten Commandments recognize the love and honor for
God as the first commandment of all. On it depend all the other commandments. Knowing that the commandments were not imposed on us for God's
pleasure, but rather for our benefit and flourishing, by insisting on God's
sovereignty, the first commandment makes our dependency on God the very
foundation of our happiness. [4]

Second, the love of God precedes whatever else we discuss in theology,
whether we speak temporally or metaphysically. For instance, love is how
we understand God, for God is love. The German Jesuit theologian Karl
Rahner (1904–1984) tells us that because God is love, God is triune, for God
needs to be in God's self more than one person in order to be love, for the
lover needs the beloved. Love also explains the creation. Again, Rahner tells
us that because God is love, God "needs" to love more than God's self. [5] For
that reason God creates us so as to enter into love with us, to bring us into his
kingdom. Love also is the ground of our redemption, for "God so loved the
world that God gave God's one and only Son, that whoever believes in him
shall not perish but have eternal life" (John 3:16). Love, too, is the way of
our sanctification, for Jesus commanded us to love God, to love our neighbor, and to love ourselves. Finally, love is our goal, for in the kingdom we
believe that we will be united forever with God and those who have gone
before us. Thus, love is our understanding of God, creation, redemption,
sanctification, and eschatological promise: inasmuch as theology is the study
of God, then love is the beginning and end of theology, for God is love.

Listen to how the First Letter of John comprehensively presents it:

> Dear friends, let us love one another, for love comes from God. Everyone who
> loves has been born of God and knows God. Whoever does not love does not
> know God, because God is love. This is how God showed God's love among
> us: God sent God's one and only Son into the world that we might live through
> him. This is love: not that we loved God, but that God loved us and sent his
> Son as an atoning sacrifice for our sins. Dear friends, since God so loved us,
> we also ought to love one another. . . .
>
> God is love. Whoever lives in love lives in God, and God in them. In this
> way, love is made complete among us so that we will have confidence on the
> day of judgment, because in this world we are like God. . . .
>
> We love because God first loved us. If anyone says, "I love God," yet
> hates one's brother or sister, that one is a liar. For anyone who does not love
> one's brother or sister, whom we have seen, cannot love God, whom we have
> not seen. And God has given us this command: Whoever loves God must also
> love their brother and sister (1 John 4:7–11, 16–17, 19–21).

It's hard to argue with this. Loving God is the foundation of the moral life.

A third reason for beginning with the love of God is that human experience confirms that, unlike freedom or truth, love drives, animates, and moves. It is what prompted the cell phone calls on September 11, 2001, the handing over of the human spirit looking for union. Not only does love look for union, but it also moves us toward freedom and truth. Love, then, makes possible our search for a freedom for greater love and a truth to love rightly.

One of the most important works in moral theology in the twentieth century specifically turned to the tradition to confirm this truth from human experience. In *The Primacy of Charity in Moral Theology*,[6] Gérard Gilleman insisted that we need an experience-based moral theology that starts at the depths of our being. He turned to charity, the love of God dwelling in us, and there he tapped into the notion of spiritual or devotional theology nourishing the depths of our spirit. When we think of charity, Gilleman, influenced by Thomas Aquinas, held that the love of God is no less than the presence of the Holy Spirit in us. Herein we find the love of God, charity animating us. Gilleman also invokes Thomas in calling charity the mother of the virtues, again because it precedes all other virtues by animating them and giving them life.

Tradition constantly confirms this human experience of the love of God preceding all else. For instance, our tradition testifies, time and again, to the love of God as the foundation of the call to become a Christian. Of course, the paradigmatic conversion marked by love is Augustine's (354–430) own. Augustine, who converted to Christianity in his early thirties, insisted on the primacy of love—"Love and do as you will." He describes in the tenth book of the *Confessions* the deeply felt, passionate, visceral pursuit of the love of God:

> Late it was that I loved you, beauty so ancient and so new, late I loved you! And, look, you were within me and I was outside, and there I sought for you and in my ugliness I plunged into the beauties that you have made. You were with me and I was not with you. Those outer beauties kept me far from you, yet if they had not been in you, they would not have existed at all. You called, you cried out, you shattered my deafness: you flashed, you shone, you scattered my blindness: you breathed perfume, and I drew in my breath and I pant for you: I tasted, and I am hungry and thirsty: you touched me, and I burned for your peace.[7]

Augustine's conversion was a response to the love of God already within him. Similarly, the conversion of St. Paul, who also testified to the primacy of love, was a call of love. Of course, unlike Augustine, we do not have from Paul the description of his conversion in quite the poetry that Augustine provided, but for the great evangelizer who wanted nothing but Christ, certainly he understood Christ's call as nothing but love.

I first came to this insight not from the Letters of Paul—though it was always there—but in a painting by Caravaggio (1573–1610). To appreciate Caravaggio's painting, I want to compare it with an earlier one by Michelangelo (1475–1564).

In Michelangelo's *The Conversion of Saul* (1542–1545), God, accompanied by angels and saints, erupts from heaven and parts the sky, allowing heaven's light to fall tornado-like on the person of Paul. God intervenes directly onto a plain, sending Paul's horse and at least fifteen soldiers away in flight. In the lower left-hand corner of the canvas, an elderly, white-bearded, stunned Paul shields his face as he turns toward the light with his companion helping him to his feet. The painting is clearly about the power of God entering dramatically and definitively into human history.

In Caravaggio's *The Conversion of Saint Paul* (1600), there are only three figures—Paul, his horse, and Paul's companion tending to the horse. On a fairly dark background we see a youthful Paul, in vibrant, passionate colors of orange, red, blue, and yellow, wearing armor, very handsome, on his back, legs opened, eyes closed. The conversion is an ecstatic moment in which Paul is purely recipient of God's love. It has a deeply erotic tone. The horse and his companion do not flee but remain standing there, neither aware of what is happening to Paul. Only Paul in his deep interiority is receiving the Lord. He is in union with the Lord. This deep, internalized conversion clearly conveys that God is doing something to Paul.

In this painting, unlike Michelangelo's, God is not visible. God is present, nonetheless, but in Paul, because someone is doing something to Paul. Caravaggio captures Paul's experience, making sure that the agent we see active is not Paul but God. Thus, even though you see God in Michelangelo's, still your eyes move to Paul. In Caravaggio's, you see Paul, but you look for God.

This move by Caravaggio is insightful. The event is not Paul being turned around. The event is Paul becoming deeply attuned to the presence of the love of God in his life. Of course, only one who has known that experience could insist that love is the only thing that lasts.

The greatness of our tradition is that the love of God is not simply the beginning of the Christian's life, but the whole continuum of it. Thus, in the Church of Maria del Popolo, Caravaggio's *The Conversion of Saint Paul* hangs in front of his *The Crucifixion of Saint Peter*. Like Paul, Peter is on his back, but his back is on a cross, and while the stimulated Paul is completely clothed, the aging flesh of Peter is fairly exposed, but hardly erotic. Peter is looking at his hands, fastened to the cross. He inevitably recalls the questioning on the beach—"Do you love me?"—and the prediction that Peter, when he is old, shall stretch forth his hands and be led where he will not want to go (John 21:15–19). Now Peter is old and about to die for Jesus Christ.

In two paintings, Caravaggio captures the beginning and the end of the Christian life as a life living out of the love of God.

THE THREEFOLD LOVE

No presentation on love can conclude without saying something about the threefold love of God, self, and neighbor. So let us consider this triad.

No contemporary moral theologian has written more on love than my former colleague Edward Vacek.[8] Vacek captures the fullness of the love of God by talking about love as *agape* (that is, the love for the beloved), love as *philia* (the love for the love or the union itself), and love as *eros* (the love that the lover experiences as lover). By bringing these together, Vacek captures the all-encompassing comprehensiveness of love.

Not surprisingly, whenever we talk about our response to God's love, we similarly use all-encompassing language. Jesus tells us that we are to love the Lord our God with our whole heart, our whole mind, our whole soul (Matt. 22:37–39). God expects nothing less and the tradition echoes that complete offering, whether in the prayer of St. Francis or St. Ignatius of Loyola's *Suscipe* (offering of oneself) prayer. Any response to the all-embracing love of God must be as exhaustively comprehensive as the offer itself. Thus the breathless love of God that Paul encounters is paralleled by the complete *Suscipe* of Peter.

Because of that comprehensiveness, Vacek argues that all persons have their flourishing in God and that if one were not to believe in God, and therefore not know the love of God, that person would be incomplete. Humans, Vacek insists, need the love of God to know the goodness of life. Without it, we are simply less.

Vacek wants to make clear, though, that the love we are to have for God is specifically for God, God's self. Vacek wants to counter those who see in neighbor love the only specific act of the love of God. In a way, Vacek hearkens us back to the preacher who sees the placard that announces "God is other people." The preacher remarks, "There is a comma missing in your sign: 'God is other, people'!"

In prayer we encounter this specific exchange of divine and human love between God and the person. Prayer is about entering into union with God specifically—about experiencing that union, about encountering the love of God. Margaret Farley talks about this expression of love as an active receptivity.[9] That active receptivity is what we saw in the Caravaggio painting of Paul: Paul is actively receiving the love of God.

The great Baroque artist Gian Lorenzo Bernini (1598–1680) caught this active receptivity when he sculpted the extraordinary ecstasy of Teresa of Avila (1515–1582). Not unlike Paul's body, Teresa's body completely succumbs to the penetrating love of God that permeates and enlivens her entire body.

Frederick Crowe described this active receptivity in another word: "complacency."[10] There he describes the first act of the beloved as resting in the love received from the lover. Complacency and active receptivity are what we see in Caravaggio's Paul and Bernini's Teresa.

Saint Ignatius of Loyola (1491–1556) is always leading us in prayer to appreciate complacency, this active receptivity. Ignatius always saw prayer as a way of receiving God, as being inflamed by God. As Ignatius directs us in prayer, he never lets us leave one scriptural passage for another, if there is still more fruit to savor.

I remember, for instance, an eight-day retreat that I began on Romans 8. I was so moved by that extraordinary chapter on hope and the Holy Spirit that when I saw my spiritual director the second day, he told me to repeat my five prayer periods on Romans 8. I enjoyed those periods and returned for each of the eight days to the same passage. Complacency is that active reception, that encounter with the indwelling of the Holy Spirit.

The genius of Ignatius is that he couples that experience of complacency with the comprehensiveness of love: he wants us to get at complacency from every imaginable angle. From meditations, colloquies, contemplations, and the applications of the senses, Ignatius wants us to see, feel, touch, hear, and taste the love of God.[11]

Like the love of God itself, prayer is an encounter with being beloved. Thus Thomas Aquinas had the great insight to write that the order of charity begins with God and moves to the self (*Summa Theologiae* II.II.26). After our encounter with the love of God, we love ourselves. God teaches us to do it, and even before we love another, we believe that by charity we love ourselves and well we should.[12]

Of course, the Gospels make this quite clear: the model for neighbor love is love of self; we are to love the neighbor as ourselves. Here is the richness of the Christian tradition on love: the love of God makes possible the love of self. And these together make possible the love of neighbor.

I think it is important to understand here a common mistake many make. Many seem to think that love of self is conditioned by whether we think of ourselves as good first. I do not want to dwell here on how good or bad we are—wait until my chapter on sin to see how "bad" I think we are—but we acknowledge in faith that while we were still sinners, God loved us (Rom. 5:8). God does not love us in our goodness; God loves us in our entirety.

I have told this story before in two other books of mine, but it is worth telling again, because in it I discovered at once what a sinner I am and how loved I am, and I felt in that same moment how much I could love myself.

From 1982 to 1987 I studied at the Gregorian University in Rome. During the summer, I would travel to either Germany or Austria for part-time study of the German language and part-time parish work. One summer, while living in Munich, I decided to go to Dachau. I wanted to go on one particular Monday, knowing that, like most European museums, the one at the camp would be closed. I wanted to go to Dachau only to pray, and I had heard that I could pray at a convent chapel that a group of religious women maintained next to the camp. In my Jesuit community in Munich, one of the members was the sisters' chaplain and he informed me that I could pray there, even on Mondays, when the camp was closed. Thus, I set out one cloudy day on my journey to pray at Dachau.

Foregoing a bus that could have taken me directly there from the train station, I walked to the camp for about three or four miles. As I walked, I became more and more angry. All I saw were nice, suburban houses with manicured lawns. I saw no trace of the tragedy of Dachau. I started asking myself, *How could anyone after 1945 live in a city called Dachau? What type of people could have a mailing address identical to the place of such persecution?* I thought that if ghosts existed, they would surely haunt this town. As I soon saw the cinderblock camp ahead of me, I wondered how anyone could claim seriously not to have known about the killings. I got closer, the skies were dark, and off to the side of the main street that led to the camp, I saw a new, white, Alpine-looking church. I thought, who are these people of Dachau who could claim that God was here in this place where they conspired to kill so many Jews, gypsies, homosexuals, and others?

I got to the camp. I was surprised by its length as I walked alongside it, and when I finally reached the end, I found the bell of the convent and rang it. I soon heard a voice telling me in German that the convent was closed. I responded that I was not a tourist, that I came only to pray. "We're closed," the German sister repeated. "I'm a Jesuit and your chaplain told me that I could pray here." "We're closed." "Can't I pray?" "We're closed; it's Monday."

I had come to Dachau to pray and was not allowed to. I began my trek back, even angrier than before. The skies were darker and my spirits were enraged. As I walked back, I saw the white church again. I thought, I did not come to pray in the church where conspirers pray; I came to pray where the persecuted died. I would not pray there in that white church.

I thought, nonetheless, that I had come to Dachau to pray. Here I had an opportunity to pray. Should I avoid the very point of my journey? I crossed the road and entered the white church. I looked up at the altar, and there I saw it. Suspended over the altar was an enormous corpus of the suffering Christ, crucified not to wood, but to the very barbed wire that the people of this town had once made for the camps. There was the suffering Christ, the Jew, and His cross had been fashioned by the Catholics of this town. They knew their guilt. And with as much speed as it took for me to see the barbed wire, I knew my guilt as well.

I had come as an innocent to pray for the dead; there in the church I saw that I was guilty.

I sat down, stunned. For one hour I sat overthrown by my own guilt, wickedness, and sinfulness. I was awash in it. And yet, I did not feel any depression. I felt, instead, light. I felt that somehow Christ wanted me to know myself, my pettiness, my selfishness, my seething judgment, and would not let me be shattered by the knowledge. I was overcome by my badness and yet Christ's strength, light, and, yes, love would not let me be lost. I felt extraordinarily vulnerable, yet oddly confident, not in me, but in Christ.

After an hour or so, I prayed for all the people that my selfishness had harmed. I begged their forgiveness, and I thanked God for this revelation of myself and of God's tender love. I left the church. Outside, I looked up, the skies were beautifully blue, with wisps of clouds across the horizon. Then a little boy passed by on his tricycle, saw me, and uttered the wonderful Bavarian greeting: "Grüss Gott!" He had just said to me, "God's greetings!" I sat down on the curb and cried. And in my tears, I realized how worthwhile it was to love God, myself, and my neighbor.

I conclude now on neighbor love. Like my experience at Dachau, we cannot love our neighbors except for as they are. I learned, in my sinfulness, by God's love, what self-love was. The comprehensiveness of love is no less applicable for neighbor love. We are called to love our neighbors, not in their goodness alone but in their entirety and in their specificity.

There are some today who try to love their neighbor by thinking of their neighbor as another Christ. But I think that is not full neighbor love: we need to love not Christ in the neighbor only, but we need also to love the neighbor. Just as we need to love specifically God and specifically ourselves, similarly we need to love specifically our neighbors as they really are. Moreover, just as we love ourselves as we really are, so too we are to love our neighbors as ourselves.

I do not want to deny that Christ may reveal to us that *after* loving our neighbor we may discover Christ, but I think that the tradition has always told the story of finding Christ in my neighbor as a lesson learned *after* the concrete act of loving the neighbor. In the Last Judgment parable in Matthew 25, we hear the sheep being told that because they fed the King, they will enter the Kingdom of God. Then they ask, "When did we feed *you*?" and the King answers, "Whenever you fed the hungry, you fed me." In the Christian tradition, St. Martin of Tours gives his cloak to a beggar in need. Later, he realizes that the beggar was Christ. But in both Matthew's Gospel and in the story of Martin, each one acts not because they see Christ, but because they see a neighbor in need. It is one thing to love Christ in Jack; it is another matter to love Jack.

I close by reflecting on prayer. For just as in prayer we encounter the love of God and the experience of active receptivity wherein we know we are loved and called to love ourselves, similarly in prayer we practice neighbor love, especially when we pray for one another. Again, in this practice we learn to love again as we enter into union with one another by lifting each other up in prayer.

We learn in prayer and from the Gospels how much God wants us to love one another, and God becomes in prayer and in life the guarantor of that love. God makes that love possible and therefore never attempts to replace that love we have for another with our love for God. When we learn lessons in love, we learn not to reduce love, but that love's nature is to extend itself, to reach beyond the self, to grasp the other, again and again, and another and another. Love is, after all, union—a deeply felt, visceral union that we keep pursuing and keep preserving in a multitude of ways, for it is so comprehensive and yet brings such complacency.

STUDY QUESTIONS

1. If you were teaching a course on moral theology, where would you start? Love? Freedom? God? Human experience? The church? Jesus Christ? Why would you start where you propose?
2. Do you think we can love God without loving our neighbor? Do you think we can love our neighbor without loving God?
3. Do you think everyone needs to love God?
4. How would you describe love?

Chapter Two

Conscience

How many times has a spouse found that the greatest trouble in a marriage is due to the other spouse's immaturity? How many pastors know that the most time-consuming difficulties they face are with a childish staff member? How many religious communities are held hostage by the expectations of one spoiled member? How many friendships are strained by the indulgent urges of someone who has never outgrown adolescence? Or better yet, let us consider ourselves. How many of us know that our worst moments result when our juvenile propensities continue to influence us?

THE CALL TO GROW

The call to be a Christian is at once a call to grow. This seemingly obvious yet healthy maxim is not, however, readily found in the long history of the moral manuals that constantly warn us against sin without urging us to grow. The call to grow is evident elsewhere: in the scriptures, in the early Fathers, in the twelfth- to fourteenth-century Scholasticism and the concurrent charismatic and religious movements, and finally again in our contemporary era.

In the New Testament, the call to follow the Lord is always understood as a call to advance. Saint Paul writes, "Forgetting what lies behind and straining forward to what lies ahead, I press on toward the goal for the prize of the upward call of God in Christ Jesus" (Phil. 3:13–14). The ever-moving Paul finds appropriate the imagery of straining forward on the way of the Lord. To the Galatians he laments their stumbling and comments "you were running well" (Gal. 5:7).

Paul's reliance on journey imagery stems from his own confirming experience of Christ, who literally manifests his love to Paul as Paul journeys toward Damascus to persecute Christ's followers. Paul is a traveler, both before and after his conversion. After meeting the risen Lord, Paul is sent on the true way. Paul's actual journeys, narrated in Luke's Acts of the Apostles, mirror the Gospel journeys of Christ, who heads for Jerusalem. They are both being called to their ultimate surrender.

Following in Jesus's footsteps is the response to the call of discipleship: the first traveler, the Lord himself, beckons each pilgrim to advance by following him. The provocative Italian film director Pier Paolo Pasolini (1922–1975) brought the journeying of Jesus to the fore in his *The Gospel According to Saint Matthew*. In that work he silhouettes Jesus as Jesus moves relentlessly across the screen toward Jerusalem, with his apostles trying desperately but rather poorly to keep up with him. Jesus is on a mission, aiming without pause to attain his destiny; everything that he does, he does as he makes haste to the Holy City. Even his Sermon on the Mount becomes a sermon on the run.

Of course, the notion of movement originates with the Gospels and not with Pasolini. The Gospels are replete with "moving" characters, seeking the Lord: the shepherds hurry to the stable as the Magi follow the star, Zacchaeus climbs a tree and Levi leaves his table, the woman with the hemorrhage pushes through the crowd and the paralytic finds the Lord by entering through a roof, the prodigal son and his father rush toward one another, Jairus and Nicodemus break ranks to see Jesus, and Cornelius visits Peter. The Gospels are filled with stories of people literally striding in their passage to the Lord.

The scripture stories were not lost on the church. The stories became the source of a new moral imperative: to advance. Gregory the Great (540–604) wrote, "Certainly, in this world, the human spirit is like a boat foolishly fighting against the river's rush: one is never allowed to stay still, because unless one forges ahead, one will slide back downstream."[1] Later, in the twelfth century, Bernard of Clairvaux (1090–1153) argued, "To not progress on the way of Life is to regress."[2] Thomas Aquinas (1225–1274) summed up their insights: "To stand on the way of the Lord is to move backwards."[3] For them, the Lord who leads us on the way expects us to move, to follow. To not follow is to retreat.

This moral call to grow is not a call to make ourselves into other gods. Certainly some have erroneously believed that by their own efforts they could become perfect, like those who ate from Eden's tree, who built the Tower of Babel, or who followed the Bishop Pelagius. But Paul helps us again: "Not that I have obtained this or am already perfect; but I press on to make it my own, because Christ Jesus has made me his own" (Phil. 3:12). The call to strive, to grow, is not a matter of choice. Rather, Christ has called us and given us the grace that commands us to respond. On God's account, we must move forward.

All this movement would be lost on us if we did not understand it as being out of love. Out of love Jesus moves to the Father in Jerusalem; out of love Paul races to the finish line; out of love Mary hastens to her cousin Elizabeth; out of love Peter and John rush to the empty tomb; out of love Mary Magdalene runs ahead to tell the disciples about the risen Lord. This call to movement, to advance, is the Christian call to grow, but to grow in love.

RIGHT GROWTH, RIGHT LOVING, AND THE PROMOTION OF THE CONSCIENCE

This call to grow in love is a summons to pursue the right way for growing. For this reason the call to growth often becomes an injunction to cultivate the virtues. By concentrating on virtues or character building, we can attend to practices that better our pilgrimage. Though virtues assist us to harness weaknesses and overcome pitfalls, their overriding function is to develop strengths. The agenda of the virtues is to promote a profoundly interpersonal and positive response to the call to grow and stands in sharp contrast to the later modern moral manuals that were so obsessed with avoiding sinful actions.

This connection between the Gospels and the virtues appears in the history of the church, not only in the patristic period but also in the great charismatic movements of the twelfth and thirteenth centuries, especially in the challenging summons of Saints Dominic (1170–1221), Francis (1181–1226), and Clare (1194–1253) to walk on the way of the Lord. Unlike their predecessors, who lived in remote monasteries, these charismatic leaders frequently left their convents to enter the newly formed urban areas and universities of the thirteenth century so as to preach the Gospel, forming religious communities precisely for that task. Telling the story of God's movement to us, they call us to move today toward God on the way of virtue.

The call to grow, the call to move forward as disciples, the call to put on virtue is always a call heard in the Christian conscience. The centrality of the personal conscience as the place for hearing the call has had a long history in the church: whenever growth and virtue are especially promoted, the conscience is also defended and promoted. During these robust periods (notably the patristic period of the first five centuries and the charismatic, religious, and Scholastic movements of the twelfth to fourteenth centuries), the primacy of the conscience is consistently articulated. Not surprisingly, then, in light of the reforms of the Second Vatican Council, which called morals to be more rooted in scripture and discipleship, the conscience again makes a vigorous appearance in contemporary moral theology.

What does Vatican II say about conscience? The definitive presentation is paragraph 16 of *Gaudium et Spes*:

In the depths of our conscience, we detect a law which does not impose, but which holds us to obedience. Always summoning us to love good and avoid evil, the voice of conscience when necessary speaks to our heart: do this; shun that. For we have in our heart a law written by God; to obey it is the very dignity of being human; according to it we will be judged (2 Cor. 6:10). Conscience is the most secret core and sanctuary of a person. There we are alone with God, Whose voice echoes in our depths (John 1:3, 14). In a wonderful manner, conscience reveals that law which is fulfilled by love of God and neighbor (Eph. 1:10). In fidelity to conscience, Christians are joined with the rest of humanity in the search for truth, and for the genuine solution to the numerous problems which arise in the life of individuals from social relationships. Hence the more right conscience holds sway, the more persons and groups turn aside from blind choice and strive to be guided by the objective norms of morality. Conscience frequently errs from invincible ignorance without losing its dignity. The same cannot be said for those who care but little for truth and goodness, or for a conscience which by degrees grows practically sightless as a result of habitual sin. [4]

There are many elements that we could pursue here—the inner sanctuary of a person, the call to do good and avoid evil, the law being fulfilled in the love of God and neighbor—but so as to explain conscience better I want to examine only three specific issues: the "voice" of conscience, the formation of conscience, and the erring conscience.

THE VOICE OF CONSCIENCE

In a seminal article forty-five years ago, John Glaser distinguished two very different voices that we hear as adults: the voices of the superego and of the conscience. The term *superego* (meaning "that-which-is-over-the-*I*") is how psychologists name that voice living in us, which, though a leftover from early childhood years, continues to assert itself throughout our lives.

When we were young children, those who cared for us instructed us on matters of safety and hygiene. Our parents through persistent guidance kept us from running in front of cars, putting our fingers into electrical outlets, playing with knives, or turning on the oven. Similarly, they taught us to keep clean, wash our hands, eat with utensils, and use the toilet. These instructions were given through voices of authority spoken with great concern and often, understandably, with tones of stress and frustration. Subsequently, these voices formed the voice of the superego.

Because they could not be omnipresent, parents and guardians needed to instill in us a voice that could supervise us even in their absence. Through constant warnings, we eventually felt their inhibiting presence restraining us from pushing a playmate in front of traffic or from exploring the many dangerous appliances in the kitchen. As children we learned that parents were always nearby. In fact, nothing could make parental control more palpably visible than when that horrendous sibling threat was uttered: "Wait 'til I tell Mom!"

Glaser calls this internalized supervising voice "a principle of pre-personal censorship and control."[5] It still lives in us today. Unfortunately, inasmuch as this voice came from people literally bigger and older than we children were, we still perceive this voice as more powerful and more authoritative than we are.

The superego was not, however, a moral guide. It was simply meant to restrain us, to keep us safe, healthy, and well. Despite whatever moral lessons parents may have given us during this time, the only thing we children really heard was that if we did not heed our parent's instructions, we would get punished. The threat—not nice moral explanations—is what we remember.

When we were wrong, we were punished, most often by being sent to our room. This is the paradigmatic form of reprimanding a child. At first we delighted in being sent away; our rebellious streak was awakened by the punishment. We thought as we stomped our way to our room, good riddance! As time passed, we would feel, however, the intended isolation and would seek permission to return to wherever the family was gathered. We would negotiate with our parents, promising never to be bad again and claiming to be contrite all along the way. Of course, we were not that upset about the wrong we had done; it was the isolation we wanted to overcome. We wanted to be back with everyone and feel loved again.

Today that same fairly standardized cyclic movement has been hardwired into our adult lives. From the superego we sense reprimand, punishment, isolation, guilt, negotiation, repentance, and acceptance. Through the superego, the cycle repeats itself time and again. We violate an accepted standard of behavior, we feel "guilty" for what we did, we apologize simply to rid ourselves of the "bad" feeling, and we are welcomed back, and we find ourselves feeling better again. Such are the mechanics of the superego.

THE FORMATION OF THE CONSCIENCE

Unlike the superego, which warns us to stay where we are, the conscience calls us to grow. For some of us, this call could mean a call to greater assertiveness. Given the call to grow, we may hear another voice warning us, "You better not do it or else you will feel guilty." That shaming voice is usually the superego. Often the conscience's calls to grow are met with threats of the superego. Even if we do decide to develop in new areas, the superego still manages to make us feel guilty and, worse, terribly isolated.

Some of us even go to our rooms, punishing ourselves exactly as our parents punished us years ago.

When I lived as a faculty-in-residence in Fordham University dorms, I saw hard-driving, bright students who, whenever they received anything less than an A, retreated to their rooms and went into a period of mourning, invariably calling their parents to be cheered up. When the superego drives us, it usually does so by threatening or punishing us, compelling us into prepubescent cyclic forms of living and acting.

Certainly this is not to say that whenever we "feel guilty," the superego and not the conscience is working. When we say things like "I feel so guilty," we should ask ourselves, "Did I do anything wrong?" If the answer is yes, then the conscience is probably judging us, but when the answer is no, the superego is probably intimidating and shaming us. Consider the case that someone has repeatedly treated us poorly. Our friends suggest, "You should speak up and tell that person to stop taking advantage of you." In conscience we recognize that this is what we should do, but the superego keeps saying, "You should be a nice person." Eventually we decide to speak up. Afterward, we may "feel guilty." This feeling is probably rooted in the superego: we went against its command to be nice and so it punished us.

Of course, the superego is not bad. After all, because of it we do not run in front of cars or play with electrical outlets, and we, thankfully, use the toilet and wash our hands. However, during our adult lives we have to live by a higher voice (the conscience) that discerns the standards of what is right and wrong. In short, we need to be vigilant about the superego so that it does not inhibit the conscience.

Moreover, by the superego we experience a certain form of social compliance. Because we are so interested in being loved, the superego threatens us with isolation and therefore hearkens us always to conformity. Conscience, on the other hand, is suspicious of conformity, particularly when injustice is at stake. Because the conscience calls us to aim more at being the one who loves than being the beloved, it prompts us often to reach out to the one that the more conformist society rejects. Moral progress, therefore, always occurs when people heed their consciences, take steps of their own, and move forward, even at the risk of isolation and loss. Consider when Rosa Parks took her place on the bus in Montgomery, when Thomas More refused to take the Oath of Supremacy, when Martin Luther King Jr. wrote to white preachers on scraps of paper in a Birmingham jail, when Gdansk shipyard workers decided to strike for their rights, when the faceless Chinese student stepped forward to meet an oncoming tank in Tiananmen Square, or when Ninoy Aquino returned to his beloved Philippines. In each instance, a person moved history and humanity forward with a conscience that demanded stepping forward where others feared to go.

Here we should never forget that the language of conscience is the force-ful language of being called, of being commanded. As *Gaudium et Spes* states, conscience "holds us in obedience"—it "summons" us. True, con-science is often used with the word *freedom*, but this is not a freedom to do whatever we want. Rather, the call for freedom of conscience is so that we are not constrained from heeding our conscience. For this reason, Christians refer to the "dictates" or the "demands" of conscience: conscience "de-mands" that we love God, ourselves, and our neighbors. Conscience "dic-tates" that we pursue justice. In fact, *Gaudium et Spes* reminds us that by the conscience we will be "judged."

When we appreciate the call of conscience, the voice to hear the demands of God, of love, and of justice, then we similarly recognize the formation of the conscience as itself a command. We need to remember, however, that forming our conscience is a lifetime process. We form it based on the wis-dom of parents, elders, and teachers, as well as friends and mentors; on the teachings and stories from the sacred scriptures, the church's tradition, and our local culture; and finally on the lessons learned in our own life experi-ence.

Many people think that forming the conscience entails learning a few laws, like the Ten Commandments. These are certainly helpful and important but we need to learn life's lessons if we want to have a formed conscience, and those lessons cannot be taught by simple commands telling us what to do and what to avoid.

The formation of conscience is like parenting oneself. We can think of how our parents helped us to begin forming our consciences, since parents form their children's consciences all the time. They teach their children to play fairly with others, to enjoy one another's company, to tell the truth, to care for siblings and friends, to take care of themselves by not eating too much or too quickly, to respect other people's property, and to be brave.

As we get older and become adults, we take over the job of forming the conscience. We learn more about the complexities of truth telling, of being faithful to friends, of acknowledging our faults, of working earnestly, of caring for the stranger, of being hospitable, and of becoming both grateful and compassionate.

I think the formation of the conscience is really a development of our relatedness in virtue: mentored practices of justice, temperance, fortitude, fidelity, and self-care through the ministration of conscience's own prudence allow us to learn more and more about how we are to respond to God, neighbor, and ourselves in love. Virtuous practices become the exercises for the formation of conscience.

The seriousness with which the church takes the conscience is seen by the way the church addresses the possible conflict between the dictates of conscience and the teaching church. What happens if my conscience tells me one thing and my church tells me something else?

This was the famous disagreement that the young Thomas Aquinas had with the famous Peter Lombard (1095–1160). Lombard's *Sentences* was the most widely used textbook (after the scriptures) of the medieval university. Every budding professor lectured on it as their first university lecture appointment. In 1252, when Thomas Aquinas first arrived at Paris to teach, he did the same. Thomas dutifully referred to Lombard as the Master, but on three occasions in his *Commentary on the Sentences*, Thomas straightforwardly rejected Lombard: "here the Master is wrong" (*hic magister falsum dicit*). Lombard had argued that one is not obliged to follow one's conscience when at odds with church teaching.[6]

We need to appreciate that the "debate" between Peter and Thomas was never settled. No pope or council ever judged that Peter or Thomas was right. Rather, in the church we live with the tension of this debate. In fact, generally speaking we believe that to form the conscience we should adhere to church teaching. We expect the conflict between conscience and church teaching to be rare. In fact, we could say that the only way we could in conscience disagree with church teaching is if our consciences took the matter so seriously that it commanded us to disagree with the church.

Still, I believe that Thomas understood the problem well: if we are not bound to what our conscience dictates as right, then we would be free to follow any fancy as morally right. But we are bound to the dictates of conscience. In fact, on Judgment Day we will have to give an account of how we lived and that account will be based on conscience. We will not be able to claim we were following others, for even the act of following is itself a conscientious action. There will be no excuses; inevitably we will render the account of how we lived and why. In being true to our lives, we will have no choice but to acknowledge how our consciences guided us throughout our adult lives. Thus, even if we believe we ought to adhere to church teaching, we do that through conscience. The conscience, then, is the seat of personal responsibility.

Following the conscience is not a private matter. On the contrary, as the seat of personal responsibility, it helps us to see that we are constitutively related to God, ourselves, and the neighbor. We are inescapably social, so much so that whatever our conscience guides us to do will be brought to light. Whatever we try to do in private will inevitably enter into the very nature of ourselves. Since we cannot escape our consciences, we cannot escape our own relational responsibilities.

Moreover, because conscience always binds, it binds even when it is erroneous; of course, no one in conscience would know that they were in error, for deliberately doing what we believe is wrong would not be acting in conscience.

Few moral teachings of the church must be followed under pain of ex-communication. Nonetheless, if the church teaches one thing and we believe in conscience something else, we are obliged to know what exactly the church teaches and whether we still have grounds for disagreement. Then we ought to know exactly what the disagreement is and how serious it is, and articulate to ourselves precisely why we are convinced that our way of acting is the more obliging way of loving God and neighbor than what the church teaches. In all of this, we must maintain a profound respect for the church's teaching and we must avoid scandalizing others. But the only reason why in this conflict we are obliged not to obey the church is because we are abso-lutely not free to violate our conscience.

Still, just because we follow our conscience does not mean that we are right. As a matter of fact, when we think about it, it is pretty easy to get things wrong. The recognition of the obligation to follow our conscience, then, does not mean that we become infallible if we heed the conscience. On the contrary, as *Gaudium et Spes* acknowledges, "conscience frequently errs."

For that reason it is important to ask the question: Do we sin when we follow a conscience in error? This question has been asked since the twelfth century, and over time we have developed different answers.

THE ERRONEOUS CONSCIENCE

I turn now to the debate on the erroneous conscience because by studying it, we can appreciate more clearly the primacy of the conscience. Moreover, by studying these different theologians we get a sense of what we mean when we say that the tradition develops. Here on the question of the erroneous conscience we see the church's theology going forward.[7]

Before we study these theologians, we need to recognize a distinction in moral theology between goodness and rightness. Goodness pertains to the person's basic moral stance. It asks: Do we love or do we strive for the right action? Rightness refers to whether the action fulfills the standards of ethics. Good people strive to get their actions right but do not always succeed. People acting out of selfishness might well do the morally right action, but since they do not act out of love, we do not refer to them as good.[8]

With these distinctions we equate badness with sin. Sin is the opposite of goodness: we can call it the failure to bother to love, a definition to which we will return in the next chapter.

Bernard of Clairvaux (1090–1153), distrusting human judgment and be-lieving that the root of sin was ignorance, exhorted his listeners to the virtue of humility and adherence to the law. Actions contrary to the law and its teaching, even though done out of ignorance, were, according to Bernard, in a word, bad. Thus, if we accept that telling a lie is always wrong, Bernard would say, if we told a lie, regardless of our motivation, we sinned.

Peter Abelard (1079–1142) thought differently. He taught that what mattered was whether we were willfully pursuing in conscience the truth. Thus, if we told a lie in conscience believing we should lie, Abelard would call us and our action good. Faced with our question, whether an action from a sincerely erroneous conscience is a sin, Bernard answers affirmatively, and Abelard negatively.

The debate between them occurred, I think, because the two great theologians were each using only one concept to describe two completely different concerns. Bernard failed to see that just because persons may do the wrong out of error, it does not necessarily mean that they are at fault and therefore sinful. He would call the action bad, even though it wasn't. Abelard wrote about moral motivation. Our motivations may be out of love and conscience, but conscience and love are no guarantee that actions will be morally right. If we willed something precisely because we thought it to be right, Abelard would call our action good. He should have called the motivation good, and the action wrong.

Think about if you were to arrive home tonight and someone met you at the door saying, "Now I have something to tell you. Before you say anything, you should know, he did it out of love." Are those "comforting" words or "warning" words? Do you think something right is actually waiting for you inside? I don't think so. Acting out of love or out of conscience is not a guarantee of right acting. Thus, whenever we hear someone say "he did it out of love" or "she meant well," we know something terribly wrong has happened, but that the person did not mean for it to be wrong. On the contrary, they were trying to find the right. Thus, if our conduct stemmed from an erroneous conscience, we may have been seeking the right, and are therefore good, but inasmuch as we were wrong, so was our action.

Later in life, Thomas Aquinas entertained the question about whether a person is good when following an erroneous conscience. Thomas's question concerned sincerity and striving: regarding the error, he asked, could one have known otherwise? For example, I believe I should enlist in the army and fight in a war. I later learn that the war was unjust. Am I responsible for my error? Thomas would ask me, could I have known the war was unjust before participating in it? If the answer was yes, then I was responsible for the erroneous conscience; if no, then I was not responsible. Thomas would call my action of enlistment wrong, but whether my action was a sin depends on whether I tried to know what I needed to know.

But what would Thomas say if I wrestled with the question of the war and then enlisted precisely because, after investigation, I believed firmly that this was a just and necessary war? Would Thomas say that though my action was wrong, I was good? Curiously, Thomas did not call the person good who, despite striving to know the right, followed an erroneous conscience; rather, Thomas argued that such a person is "excused" from blame.

Later, William of Ockham (1285–1347) adopted Thomas's argument on the primacy of the conscience but added that one who exercises the conscience responsibly, even if it is erroneous, receives merit. Ockham, unlike Abelard, recognized that ignorance is sometimes blameworthy but, like Abelard, he recognized the goodness of an erroneous conscience acting in good faith.

Certainly by the sixteenth century most moral theologians agreed with Thomas—that a dictate of conscience must be followed and that an erroneous conscience in good faith is, at least, excused from blame. In fact, by the end of the seventeenth century in 1690, Pope Alexander VIII condemned all those who taught that an invincibly ignorant conscience did not, at least, excuse. (Implicitly, Bernard's attack on Abelard is rejected.)

In the eighteenth century, Alfonso Liguori (1696–1787), later the patron saint of moral theologians, developed a new position on erroneous conscience: if a person acted out of love and/or charity when committing error, then not only is the person excused, but the person is good. Whereas Ockham described the person's striving as meritorious, now Liguori, in many ways the master of the moral manuals, asserts the person's goodness.

In the nineteenth and twentieth centuries, the moral manualists endorsed Liguori's teaching. For instance, in speaking of when a person acting from an erroneous conscience would be good, they gave the specific example of lying to protect someone. Thomas's hesitancy to describe any wrongdoer as good was overcome by Liguori and adopted by his successors. In 1953, Francis Connell, the dean of the Catholic University of America in Washington, DC, wrote that if a person acts out of an erroneous conscience, though the action is certainly not per se willed by God, "God will reward him for sincerely following his conscience."[9]

CONCLUSION

What can we conclude about this development of theological opinion on erroneous conscience? First, the description of the sincere but ignorant conscience as bad is justly condemned by Pope Alexander VIII.

Second, to describe erroneous actions as "good" is likewise rejected. Trying to find the right is no guarantee of eventual success.

Third, some may feel inclined to accept Thomas's description of the person as "excused." But today we use "excused" to describe a person who is victimized by some external cause that diminishes the ability to will and act. Thus, under the control of mental illness, drugs, threats, and so on, a person would be "excused" from blame today, if that control resulted through no fault on the person's part.

If a person has been first acting out of love or out of conscience, searching to find the right, then the person is good. Unlike being coerced or drugged, a person who errs in good faith is a person who has struggled to find the right, searched heart and mind, and in firm good faith and free will acted with conviction, albeit in error. This person is good, and what differentiates this person from another who strives in the same way but whose conduct is recognized as right is precisely the evaluation of the conduct as wrong. Calling the conduct wrong is the sufficient negative description for the activity of the erroneous conscience.

One evident instance where getting things right is an arduous and unlikely event is parenting. This vocation requires getting things right for oneself as well as for one's children, who themselves are unpredictable. Thus, in teaching children responsibility, parents often miss the mark. But why? Do parents err because they were, at that moment, less loving or less conscientious? Or do they err from a lack of experience, or foresight, or, let us say, perfect knowledge?

When a parent tries to get things right, he or she may fail. But does that failure result from the parent loving less? The parent was wrong, admittedly, but in the care and striving to do the right, to help and instruct the child, was the parent less loving? If there was no diminishment in the striving for the right, there was no diminishment in the moral goodness. Thus calling the conduct wrong does not mean that the parent was any less good or loving than another who strove equally as much and gave the right guidance.

Still, you may not want to draw the same conclusions. Such hesitancy may result from two objections. The first, you may be thinking: "Are you saying that Hitler, because he may have acted out of conscience, was not bad?" But we have to ask, do we really believe that Hitler was striving as much as possible to find the right? Do we really believe that, in a world that has taught for centuries that injustice is wrong and has tried to elucidate the most minimal insights into justice, Hitler's activities were simply mistaken and sincere interpretations of justice? Can we really believe a scenario in which the Holocaust is the thinking of a person who was striving to be right? Certainly the access we have to any of the discussions leading to his decisions hardly supports such a belief. In a word, the Hitler question only proves our insight: not only was Hitler's conduct wrong, but his motivations were bad or evil. In the case of Hitler, his evident failure to strive for justice was so appallingly clear that we rightfully call him bad. As Iris Murdoch writes, "we have not recovered from . . . the experience of Hitler."[10] But Hitler and other unjust dictators aside, the contemporary reflection on erroneous conscience helps us to see something often overlooked: the failure to act rightly does not result necessarily from a failure to act out of conscience.

Still, some may want to keep Thomas's evaluation for another reason. After all, our record (as individuals and as a people) for getting things wrong is strikingly high. With such a record we are wary of any device that could diminish our efforts. We sense that if we start calling these well-meaning wrongdoers good, we'll let them off the hook.

But is it not more often the case that the last people to let themselves "off the hook" are precisely those who strive for rightness out of love and yet err? When we do something wrong, we should call our action wrong; but when we act out of love, we should realize we are good. Giving credit where credit is due is, after all, a step in the right direction. [11]

STUDY QUESTIONS

1. If we agree that the call to be a Christian is the call to grow, what does the call to grow look like?
2. How would you define the conscience?
3. Are you able to distinguish superego from conscience? Give an example of when you confused the conscience with the superego.
4. Over the past year, what lessons in life did you learn that helped you to form your conscience?
5. Explain whether you would call a person good who strives for the right out of love but fails.

Chapter Three

Sin

Through a series of steps I want to wear down some long-standing presuppositions that we have about sin. Then I want to propose a new notion of sin.

When I was about seven years old, like other Brooklyn Catholics, I already knew a great deal about my faith. We studied the Baltimore catechism and were tested weekly. We had May crownings, the feast of all saints when we dressed as our namesakes, first communions, confirmations, and Friday benedictions (where, along with "Tantum Ergo," we sang "An Army of Youth"). My mother was in the Rosary Altar Society, my father was in the Knights of Columbus, and I was an altar boy. We knew Latin, understood what a maniple was, and kept a sacrament of the sick kit at home. We were Roman Catholic.

While most of the time being a Roman Catholic was an uplifting experience, it was when sin and confession were introduced into our lives that we came into contact with what philosophers call "existential anxiety." Probably the greatest anxiety circled around making a good confession or, rather, failing to make one.

I remember walking to school with a seven-year-old classmate considering the case of someone who forgets to tell all their sins in one particular confession and then the next time goes to confession and forgets to tell those sins yet again and how all the subsequent confessions would be bad, just as the first one was. I feared it happening to me. I remarked to my friend, "And how could I ever remember to redo all those confessions?" Then, just as we were about to cross the street, in the middle of my angst-ridden monologue, my friend shared with me his ultimate fear: "Just imagine being hit by a car and not being in the state of grace!"

Catholic life in the late 1950s had a certain give and take. You always felt the give, but you also felt the take, and sin and hell were the takes. We worried about sin and confession a lot.

At one point I learned what a mortal sin was and how we commit it. It needed to be a grave act, committed with full knowledge and full consent of the will. These seemed to me to be significant conditions. After one Sunday mass I was walking home with my grandmother when I asked, "Grandma, I've been thinking about mortal sin. Who could ever do something really big and wrong, really mean it, and really want to do it? It just seems awfully hard to do all three." "You're right, Jimmy. It's very hard to commit a mortal sin." No more consoling words could have been spoken.

Not surprisingly, years later I became a moral theologian. In my years of study, I found a text that contradicted my grandmother. It was in Thomas Aquinas's *Summa Theologiae*. He asked whether St. Peter sinned mortally when he denied Christ. Thomas's answer was remarkable. But before reading his answer, consider what your answer to the question might be: grave matter, full knowledge, and full consent. Did Peter sin mortally? He was denying Christ. That was definitely grave matter. Did he have full knowledge, however? With a lot of anxiety pumping through Peter, could he fully understand what he was really being asked? Did he have the presence of mind to recognize the gravity of his sin? Furthermore, could he possibly have had full consent? Certainly, he did not want to be in that situation; he did not want to deny Jesus. Could we ever call his consent "full"? Without full knowledge and full consent, could Peter have sinned mortally?

Yes, says Thomas. Peter's denial was a mortal sin. He could have said he was Jesus's friend. He did not; therefore, Thomas argues, he had full knowledge and full consent. Thomas saw full consent and full knowledge not as separate conditions but rather as parts of the entire composite scene. Thomas did not use these conditions to exonerate as we do today; he used them to illustrate that the sin was mortal. In other words, he interpreted full knowledge and full consent differently than we do, not looking for what was missing but rather recognizing what was there. Peter knew otherwise and could have acted otherwise; therefore there was knowledge and consent.

Thomas was a positive realist when it came to the human condition. He believed that we are capable, intelligent, and free and therefore competent with our moral lives. He also held that we often act without responsibility for our lives and actions. For this reason, he believed we frequently sinned mortally.

So how do we arbitrate my grandmother's insight that we hardly ever sin mortally with Thomas's that we frequently sin mortally? As much as I hate to say it, Thomas is basically right; my consoling grandmother was, like so many, a bit indulgent.

Perhaps the word *mortal* is a bit daunting when speaking of degrees of sin, but I think anyone who looks at the history of the way we have talked about sin would see that we have become an incredibly self-excusing people of God. We have managed to move from the assumption that generally, when we act, we act with knowledge and consent to the present habit of acquitting one another from culpability by claiming lack of knowledge and consent.

Anyone who has done any therapy, for instance, knows the importance of claiming responsibility for one's actions. It is not morally, spiritually, or psychologically healthy to relinquish our competency. (Let me note, here, that I have not yet talked about what I mean by sin, but my first point is to rescue human freedom and responsibility from the present tendency to acquit too readily.)

HOW BAD ARE WE?

I believe one reason why we so frequently acquit is because we do not want to face how morally bad we actually are. Like most medieval theologians, Thomas believed that we frequently fail to exercise our moral responsibilities and that therefore most of us are going to hell. The medieval phrase that captured this belief was *massa damnata*, the "damned masses." Thomas did not invent this unhappy phrase. Augustine created it eight hundred years earlier, and, in fact, from the fourth to the twentieth century many, many church members believed it as well.

For some reason, somewhere around the 1960s, just as I was walking with my grandmother in Brooklyn, we began talking about God's universal offer of salvation and mercy, and we began doubting the phrase *massa damnata*. In the scriptures we began finding explicit and implicit assurances of the universal offer of salvation. Maybe we were sinners, but God was merciful toward all who called on God.

A generation after that we adapted our beliefs yet again. We began seeing that not only was God's merciful offer of salvation for all, but we also started to claim that God's creation was good and that because humanity was in God's image, we were especially good.

These assertions are true, certainly, but the biblical affirmation of our goodness as created in God's image is very different from the claim that in living out our lives we are morally good. Nonetheless, we went from the first goodness to the second with considerable ease and replaced the *massa damnata* with the *massa bona*. With uncommon frequency, in the 1970s, 1980s, and 1990s, we heard people preaching how good we are, how we all are surely going to enter God's kingdom, and so on. That is, rather than reminding ourselves we were sinners, but saved, we simply declared that we were good.

Curiously, many, many people stopped going to the sacrament of confession. Seventeen hundred years of sermons warning us that we could be among the majority of people going to hell was certainly an incentive for at least trying to be among the lucky minority. Now, after thirty years of sermons contradicting the earlier claims, we no longer feel the intimidation that prompted our frequent entries into the confessional box. Moreover, by insisting that we are so good, we are left with the inevitable question: if we are so good then why do we need confession?

Of course, we need to pause. Were theologians and preachers actually wrong for seventeen centuries in their presupposition regarding the *massa damnata*? I think they were as wrong as those who argue the contrary today. I think knowing the state of ourselves on Judgment Day is not in the purview of human estimation. Since in Matthew 25 all the sheep and all the goats had no idea of how their judgment day would be, I see no reason for despair or presumption about how our Judgment Day is going to turn out. It eludes us, and rightly so. In short, I think we need to tone down whatever "certainty" we have on either claim.

In a manner of speaking, previous generations recognized our sinfulness but failed to see the gift of grace, mercy, and salvation. The masses may have been sinful, but whether they were damned is another question. The dying words of Christ—"forgive them for they know not what they do" (Luke 23:24)—were not uttered solely for those standing on Golgotha. They have everlasting significance. We may not be the *massa damnata*, but we are evidently not the *massa bona* either. We are the sinful masses, saved. In a word, we are sinners, but loved.[1]

SINNING OUT OF OUR STRENGTH

I want to pose another question: do we really sin out of our strength or out of our weakness? As one who hears confessions, I am always struck by how people confess their weaknesses repeatedly. Wherever we are weak, we confess it: I lost my temper; I failed to stand up to my boss; I drank too much. . . . We confess where we are weak.

Not only that, we actually spend quite a bit of moral effort striving to overcome or subdue the particular weakness. We confess: I struggle with my anger; I struggle with my lack of courage; I struggle with my drinking. Most of us expend most of our moral energy on our weaknesses. Predictably, at some point we fall short of our goals. And at that point we think we sin, and we confess yet again where our weakness is, where we failed, where we did something wrong.[2]

Of course, the area in our life where many of us are most complicated is in our sexuality. And, not surprisingly, where we have all sorts of weaknesses, we are constantly confessing. Where you and I are weak, messy, and broken, we believe we sin. In those same areas we expend great moral effort and yet we name that part of our lives as our sinfulness. Where we are weak, we sin. Or so we think.

Let me be clear. I think that when we suffer from moral weaknesses and do not try to overcome them, *then* we sin. But my experience tells me that many people are very attentive to their weaknesses and actually try to keep them in check, but they still fail. Are they sinning if they try as much as they can?

I think that focusing on our weaknesses allows us to avoid the real understanding of sin. By focusing on our weaknesses, we focus on the areas of our life where we feel impoverished and where we really believe that we are not as strong as it may seem. By focusing on our weaknesses, we inevitably believe that we are weak—good, but weak. If only I was stronger, we think. But do we really, primarily, sin out of our weakness? I do not think so.

As the medieval theologians understood well, every narrative in the Gospel is not about sinners sinning out of their weaknesses, but out of their strengths. When the publican and the Pharisee are praying in the temple, the sin of the Pharisee is in his strength (Luke 18:9–14). He specifically considers what he has. When the rich man steps over Lazarus and ignores Lazarus at the gate and in need, the rich man's sin is not in his weakness, but in his strength (Luke 16:19–31). He could have done something; he did not—he sinned, precisely out of his strength. The steward who asked forgiveness for his debt is forgiven, but he's punished because he does not forgive the minor debt by his own employee (Matt. 18:21–35). Out of his strength, the steward is convicted. Think of the parable of the Good Samaritan—where is the sin? Even the robbers who committed the crime of beating the poor man on the road to Jericho are ignored. The focus is on the Levite and the priest; they could have acted, but they did not (Luke 10:25–37). They sinned precisely out of their strength. Or think of the Last Judgment. Note how the sheep and goats are separated—by what they could have done and whether they did it (Matt. 25:31–46).

Is it not odd, then, that the entire Gospel tradition has us sinning out of our strengths, and yet we think that we sin out of our weaknesses? But notice too that we have the same problem here as we did with my consoling grandmother: a certain self-understanding where we tend to think of ourselves as weak, as without knowledge, without freedom, without consent, whenever we consider ourselves as sinners. Why is that? Why do we think of ourselves as weak when we think of ourselves as sinners?

I think it is a fairly natural instinct, but I think it is profoundly self-deceptive. Not surprising, right? Is not the nature of sin to be self-deceptive, and would not our instinct be to deceive ourselves about the nature of our sinfulness? Because of this, we need to keep our eyes on the scriptures, because they help us be aware of at least two truths: that we are probably greater sinners than we admit and that we sin out of our strength.

SURPRISED BY SIN

But let us look to the scriptures again. How well do people know of their sinfulness? In the Gospel stories people are surprised to find out how sinful they are. This is extraordinary. Think for instance of the Last Judgment again. The goats ask, "But when did we not feed you? When did we not visit you?" They are clueless about their self-understanding as sinners. Similarly, the rich man is ignorant of his impending fate. He did not know he'd go to hell for not caring for Lazarus. Listen to him: "Father Abraham, tell my brothers," he pleads from Hades. Or what about the priest and the Levite who pass the wounded man in the Good Samaritan parable? Do they see what we see, that they have failed to be neighbors? Do we see anywhere within the parable someone stopping them and telling them, "Hmm, you two better realize that you just sinned by passing by the wounded man on the road"? Or again, the Pharisee with the publican. Does the Pharisee know the judgment of arrogance being attributed to him in his prayer? I'm always surprised at how dense the scriptural characters are about the state of their souls: they do not recognize their sinfulness. So why do we think that we are any different?

DOMESTICATING AND TRIVIALIZING SIN

Not only do we think we know our sinfulness, but we actually try to put sin into nice, discreet, manageable categories: we can confess our sin, its kind, and its number. In little packages, we tidily wrap up our sins and present them for confession. John Mahoney in *The Making of Moral Theology* studies our tradition of confessing sins and argues that we have "domesticated" our sinfulness.[3]

"I got angry at my spouse three times, I lied once, I wasn't honest on my taxes, I missed mass on Sunday, I committed adultery once." Let us just stop and think about that anger for a moment. Just one of the times . . . let us try to take it in. What was it about, how long did it last, how many people did we exclude in order to demonstrate our anger, who was affected, how much, to what extent? Let us do a meditation on each of these sins that we so nicely named, categorized, numbered, and confessed.

After that meditation, let us ask ourselves whether we even scratched the surface of our sinfulness. The nature of sin in the Gospel is, after all, pervasive, deceptive, and elusive. Have we learned that? Have we not seen constantly in the Gospels how hard it is to know of one's sinfulness, let alone how impossible it is to subdue sin and then to name it and present it according to kind and number?

We have domesticated sin, and in domesticating sin we have trivialized it, as Mahoney notes. We tuck sin into nice prepackaged categories. But in order to trivialize sin, we need the evident ones, the ones on the surface, the obvious ones or the easy-to-name ones. So we say, "I got angry three times."

Our weak sins are also the ones that we really work hard at. These sins do not highlight our coldness of heart, our mean-spiritedness, our pettiness, our deep-seated resentfulness, our sinfulness. When we name our "weak" sins, we claim simultaneously that we struggled, that we sincerely made an effort, that we were, after all, vulnerable and excusable.

But we have deep within us some incredible, hidden sinfulness. Albert Camus (1913–1960) recognized our secret sinfulness in his great work *The Plague*.[4] Telling the story of a people suddenly infected by a plague, Camus conveys the greatness and the smallness of the people of the great city of Oran, who respond gracefully and wickedly to the crisis. But as suddenly as the plague came, equally suddenly it recedes. The people who were once completely unaware of how deeply vulnerable they were to a plague learn during the epidemic how foolish they were. When the plague disappears at the end, the people breathe a sigh of relief. All the plague has done is recede into hiding; the citizens think that they are safe, that they have subdued it, but they have not. And they have forgotten how vulnerable they are.

Of course, the plague was a metaphor. For Camus, the real plague was the deep-rooted selfishness of people, which showed itself so manifestly throughout World War II. During the war, while a few were heroic, many simply avoided their neighbor; they avoided responding to their neighbor in need. Instead, they collaborated and protected only themselves. As in the plague, in the war people showed how they really only think of themselves.

We should look at this from another angle. In my introductory course on moral theology I have my students read a brilliant essay titled "Self-Deception and Autobiography," by David Burrell and Stanley Hauerwas.[5] The authors examine the life of Albert Speer (1905–1981), a promising architect, who sought acceptance, whose talent was recognized by Adolf Hitler, and who was eventually brought by Hitler into his own entourage. Hitler commissioned Speer to be the architect of Nuremburg and Berlin.

Speer was a "nice" man, a family man. He had none of the incredibly vicious, hate-driven obsessions that many leaders of the Third Reich (like Goebbels, Goering, and Himmler) possessed. He was basically a man interested in his architectural work, his career, and his family. He also was attracted to fame.

He was incredibly efficient. His efficiency assisted the Reich considerably when he was made minister of armaments in 1943. Then he developed a way to get munitions to the front lines of the somewhat-collapsing Nazi forces and thus protracted the war by nearly two years. It was not the treacherous thugs and the bigots who empowered the Nazis during the last years of their disgusting war—it was someone who did not share their ideology, someone who had no ideology, someone who did not hate. He loved, but only himself and his family, and certainly not the stranger or the marginalized. He did not bother to love. He was simply someone who was efficient, who did the work well because he enjoyed having Hitler's confidence and architectural commissions. He traded his efficiency for fame, recognition, and contracts. He was a modern-day Faust.

Burrell and Hauerwas suggest that when we think of sinning we should think of Speer rather than Hitler or one of his gang, because chances are that we are more capable of becoming a Speer than a Hitler. Sure, Hitler sinned, and he sinned in remarkable ways, but the sin of Speer is more ordinary, more familiar, more likely. It fits in with that haunting insight of Hannah Arendt about the "banality of evil." Give us the right place, the right time, the right conditions, and it may not take us much to become a Speer. We are all subject to the plague, no?

The sin of Speer is not in what he did, but in what he did not do. He did not murder, torture, or rape; he did not even hate or inflame passions. For Speer conveyed himself to others in such a way that his subordinates did not even approach him with news of Nazi atrocities. Besides being efficient and seeking Hitler's approval, the only other activity Speer tried was not knowing what the Nazis were doing. He would not want his life or his family's disturbed. In a word, he simply did not bother himself with news of the monstrosities that the Nazis were performing. And as minister of armaments this was not easy avoidance, for he was directly responsible for the horrible "labor" camps.

I want to suggest that, as a matter of fact, the real reason why we are more likely to become a Speer than a Hitler is because, like Speer, we do not want to see our sinfulness, we are presumptuous about our goodness, and we do not think we are wicked. In fact, like Speer, we think of ourselves as different from those, like Hitler, who hate. We think when we sin we are weak, and we deliberately underestimate what we could have done.

But where is sin, then? How can we name it so as to appreciate how pervasive and deceptive it is? How can we recognize its strength in our strength and its affinity to our own hidden humanity?

SIN AS THE FAILURE TO BOTHER TO LOVE

To capture the breadth, depth, and pervasiveness of sin, I propose that sin is simply the failure to bother to love. That is it. This definition of sin is a biblical one: it captures the sin of Matthew's goats, Lazarus's rich man, the wounded man's priest and the Levite, the publican's Pharisee, and so on. Each of the Bible stories that refers us to sin refers us to what one could have done and did not do. Not only the stories that we have looked at, but others as well: the man who did not invest the talent (Matt. 25:14–30), the virgins who were not vigilant (Matt. 25:1–13), the son who did not go into the field to work as he said he would (Matt. 21:28–32). Sin is in the failure to bother to love.

Our sin is usually not in what we did, not in what we could not avoid, not in what we tried not to do. Our sin is usually where you and I are comfortable, where we do not feel the need to bother—where, like the Pharisee, or even Speer, we have found complacency, a complacency not where we rest in being loved but where we rest in our delusional self-understanding of how much better we are than others. It is at that point of self-satisfaction that—like Speer, the Pharisee, the prodigal's older brother, or the rich man—we usually do not bother to love.

Let us look at this notion of sin as a failure to bother to know from another point of view. While teaching at Fordham University, I lived in the dorms with the undergraduates. For several years, I lived with sophomores. These people were now familiar with the lay of the land, had gotten over homesickness, and were pursuing their own adult identities. They were a lot of fun. I particularly enjoyed noticing how they talked about their parents. In the beginning of the year, the students often described their parents as Joe and Jackie Cool, in part to win the interest of new friends. But as acquaintances and friendships developed, they started talking about the ways that their parents missed the mark. In a way, they made their parents their competitors: they were not going to make their parents' same mistakes.

They divided their parents' mistakes into two categories. First, there was the "my mom and dad can be a pair of klutzes." These were harmless but humorous accounts that usually centered on simple accidents or mistakes: Mom making a wrong turn or Dad forgetting something important. Of course, they were greatly embellished and sometimes complete fabrications. But through them, these nineteen-year-olds could feel slightly superior to their absent (and undefended) parents.

The other descriptions of parental mistakes were not humorous, nor were they disclosed as publicly. These were rather confidential disclosures between roommates, friends, or lovers. They were painful private accounts—probably a lot truer than the comic public ones—about how shortcomings in one parent affected the life of this particular daughter or son. They were tales of a parent who drank too much, who worked hard but flew off the handle in anger, or who was too timid to communicate adequately with a spouse, employer, or child. In any event, these were long-running accounts of how a particular parent's own shortcomings hurt this particular child.

Curiously, the students soon began evaluating these mistakes. They dismissed the first set as simple error. But they eventually wanted to know whether the harm caused by the second set meant that their parent did not love them. They wanted to figure out whether they meant anything to the overworked, underconfident, obsessive parent. Assuredly their parent was wrong for drinking too much, blowing a fuse, or hiding out, but was that wrongness a sign that the parent did not love? Curiously, the students probably did their best moral reasoning as they wrestled with this key question.

Eventually, they were able to see that there was a distinct possibility that the parent may actually have been trying so hard at being a good parent precisely when the personal problems erupted. Appreciating their parent as limited and recognizing their parent as capable of causing considerable harm at times, they still saw that the parent may well have been trying to overcome the timidity, wrestle with the demon, or tame the anger, and, despite the attempts, still failed. In fact, they could go so far as to recognize in the parent's attempt to resist the weakness, the desire of the parent to be as loving as possible. The parent was wrong, but not because she did not bother to love.

This insight was often matched by another student, long silent, with neither the comic nor sad stories of parental shortcomings. That student could remark that for him nothing went wrong, childhood had no crisis, and the parent was neither a klutz nor dysfunctional. As a matter of fact, he was given a good deal, or so he thought. But now, listening to the struggles of his friends' parents, he was not sure that his own parents ever loved him, ever bothered with him. Could life have been so routinely facile that the parents never bothered to love? The moment that this fear was raised, students knew that they were facing something terribly profound about human life. For not only were they faced with a peer who was uncertain about his parents' love, but they were also glimpsing that key insight that we saw in the last chapter: we can never simply presume from right or wrong activity that one is good or bad, loving or not.

If we want to know what sin is, these students' insights are terribly instructive. Who is the sinner in these narratives? The parents who tried to be caring, responsible, and loving, yet caused harm, or those who did well but loved little? Clearly, I think sin is more in the latter than in the former. This is, after all, the point we arrived at in the last chapter.

LEARNING TO CONFESS OUR SINFULNESS

We saw in the last chapter that a good conscience—that is, a conscience that strives for the right—does not guarantee that the action will in fact be right. Therein is the distinction in moral theology between goodness and rightness.

Now we are looking through another perspective at the same distinction, here as it relates to badness and wrongness. All our weaknesses, all our failings are clearly instances of our wrongness, where you and I fall short of the mark—where we hurt others, even when we try not to. But we've been trying to get to sin, which is badness, not wrongness.

If the real moral measure of our lives is moral goodness—that is, where we love, where we strive for the right—then sin is its opposite—where we are bad, where we fail to bother to love. Just as it is difficult to know where there is goodness, similarly it is hard to know where there is sin. Sin is, as it is in the parents of the sophomore, in coldness of heart. And it takes a while to find where the heart is cold.

But that coldness is what we find in all the Gospel stories that speak of sin: the goats, the rich man, the priest, the Levite, the Pharisee, the virgins, even the older unforgiving brother of the prodigal—all of them are basically thoughtless and coldhearted. But they are also, as we've seen, blind to their coldheartedness, to their wickedness, to their sinfulness. Their blindness is rather remarkable.

Think for a moment of the complacency of the older brother of the parable of the prodigal son: he does not see any wrongdoing that he's done. His brother's wrongdoing is not his. His brother has broken the law; he has not. Not seeing any wrongdoing of his own, he acquits himself of any badness. He believes that his brother does not deserve the celebration; on the contrary, in all his pettiness the older brother thinks he deserves the celebration. The Pharisee does the same thing: he sees the publican and the publican's wrongdoing. In that light he sees that he has done no wrong, and, like the prodigal's older brother, he acquits himself of badness. None of these see their own coldheartedness, these hearts that fail to bother to love: not the priest, nor the Levite, nor the goats.

We are a little different. We obsess about our wrongdoing and fret about our weakness and confess our vulnerability. Where we struggle over our wrongdoing, we name it as sin. But is not sin in fact where we do not struggle, where we do not bother to love? Sin is not in our weakness; it is in our strength. It is where, like the older brother, we are complacent—not in the sense that we rest in being loved, but that we believe we have measured up, that we are just fine, that, like all the other New Testament sinners, we are satisfied with ourselves.

If sin is very deceptive, if sin is hidden, if it is not where we have evident weakness but where we are strong, how can we confess it? At least we can name our wrongdoing. How do we name our failure to bother to love?

The late Swiss moral theologian Franz Böckle (1921–1991) talks about the effectiveness of confession. What he means is, if we do not confess our sinfulness, we never recognize our sinfulness. But, if we acknowledge our moral faults, we discover the depths of our faults. In fact, as we confess, we learn more and more about our sinfulness.[6]

I find it helpful here to consider times when we have had a very unfortunate argument with a loved one. Afterward, as we revisit the dispute, estranged from our loved one, we live in our own heads, where we keep playing tapes about the other being at fault, about our being innocent and their being responsible to seek reconciliation. If the moment of reconciliation ever begins, if we ever start talking to the other, however, we often find ourselves readily admitting that, as a matter of fact, we may have erred; it may have been our fault too. In other words, when we begin speaking with a willingness to acknowledge our own faults, our tapes change and we become more able to recognize the situation for what it was.

Böckle then suggests that when you and I begin to recognize our sinfulness, Christ's light often shines on us to let us see how much we have sinned and to see how we could have loved. Until we begin to recognize our sinfulness, we really cannot understand it. This is, of course, Ignatius's insight for the first week of the *Spiritual Exercises*. There, in the light of God's merciful love, we learn how we are sinners but saved.

I think that the confession of sin, however, is not an itemized list. Certainly there may be some wrong actions that were sinful that were evident absences of love. But we must be careful that, in naming our wrong actions, we do not deceive ourselves into thinking that we have subdued and domesticated our sinfulness, that we have recognized our badness, that we have captured the pervasiveness of where we have not loved.[7] I think real confession, tasting the real fruit of the sacrament of reconciliation, is found when we try to name not only the wrong we have done but also the ways we have not loved. There we encounter a simple resigned sense that we are quite capable of being much more loving persons than we are. It is an encounter with our extraordinary propensity to arrogance, self-sufficiency, and moral narcissism. It is where we come into contact with our badness, our self-complacency. But, interestingly, we can only do it with the love of Christ; his mercy lets us see it.

SOCIAL SIN

This definition of sin as the failure to bother to love takes a lot of individualism out of sin, because it highlights the call to love and therefore acknowledges the many ways that we are all related.

This notion of sin then is compatible with social sin. In fact, this notion of sin gives those who support the concept of social sin an even greater claim on us, simply because such a notion of sin would have to be inevitably social: if sin is the failure to bother to love, what sin would not be social?

All sin is social. Wherever people are suffering, we need to ask ourselves, are we adequately attuned to their needs? But that question leads us to another question. If sin is pervasive and deceptive, then we cannot simply ask ourselves whether we are adequately attuned to their needs, because inevitably there will be something in our society that will keep us from knowing about the needs of those for whom we are responsible. This is, of course, how Hauerwas's Albert Speer, Camus's France, and Matthew's goats managed not to sense the call to love those who were near them: society provided them with blinders from recognizing what they needed to know. And we can be as sure that our societies, just as my grandmother did, routinely acquit us from the moral responsibility for the way we live and the effects our lives have on others. We live in societies that do not want us to be disturbed.

In his "Letter from Birmingham City Jail," Martin Luther King Jr. (1929–1968) wrote not to outright racists; rather, he wrote to white preachers (not unlike Albert Speer) who should have known better about the Gospel's call to love and mercy, but who instead became complacent with a white racist society. King asks, why were they so comfortable when the Gospel was so clear? He recognizes that the societies we live in anesthetize us from the conscience that prompts us to ask if we bother to love.[8]

As a boy living where I did in Brooklyn and later living on eastern Long Island, I never thought of racism. I never thought that there were any barriers for black people. As a boy, I never knew black people and while I thought (and heard) that people in the South were racists, I never thought we were. My society isolated me from thinking that maybe I was a participant in a strategy that was actually exclusive and deeply racist.

How would I learn to think otherwise? I learned to listen to some of my teachers, especially the nuns. They helped me, hard as it was, to learn to ask questions and to think outside the box, to realize that life was more complicated than I thought and that some people really were victims of some pernicious but unspoken policies. They invited me to assume another perspective.

When I began to understand my society and my neighborhood better, I began to see how I fit comfortably into a pattern of benefits and goods that were excluded from others. From there I began to appreciate that it is not until we begin to see the other side that we begin to understand our own much better.

Years later, after entering the Jesuits, I was given a lot more opportunities to learn more about life. During my second summer in the novitiate I had a job to locate all the migrant camps in a nice, family-values county in upstate New York. Working with another Jesuit, we drove more than one hundred miles a day to find one camp after another. The incredible hardships of these people were literally hidden from the "good" Christians of the town. Yet the town prospered because of the work of these poor people. Farmers could not have profited without the cheap labor of these nearly enslaved migrant workers. I remember listening to the workers' stories, about their debts to their bosses, about their lack of ownership of any tangible goods, about their constant movements from New York to Florida and back, following crop seasons but always involved in back-breaking work. How would they ever get out of this cycle of poverty? They were trapped.

Later I would see the same set of divisions, where people were trapped on the other side, whether in tenements in New York or garbage heaps in Manila. People were literally stuck in their situation and the structures of society wanted them to be there. But rarely did people on the other side of the division see how profoundly unjust and dehumanizing these structures were.

Years ago, in 1932, American theologian Reinhold Niebuhr (1892–1971) wrote about this phenomenon in *Moral Man, Immoral Society*. He argued that individuals can be motivated by a sense of compassion and justice, but that societies are not capable of such transcendence. On the contrary, societies resist understanding their hypocrisy, their oppressive structures, and their need for reform. In fact, they promote, through a variety of forums, a complacency in their members, subtly coaxing people from seeing the world in which we actually live.

Movies love to look at this disturbing reality. In *The Truman Show*, Jim Carrey plays a character locked into a TV show by media manipulation, thoroughly unaware that reality is beyond the stage set. In *Pleasantville*, Joan Allen, Tobey Maguire, and Jeff Daniels play people trapped in a 1950s-like society that has no diversity, no emotional life, and no color. What they cannot see, they cannot understand. In *Far from Heaven*, Dennis Quaid, Julianne Moore, and Dennis Haysbert live in the 1950s society that prided itself on moral standards that kept them from facing the oft-hidden issues of race, love, and sexuality. In *The Island*, Ewan McGregor and Scarlett Johansson live in a near-perfect society of order and control, dreaming of winning the lottery that includes a trip to the island. But these dreamers do not know that they are merely clones whose body parts will be harvested when they win the lottery. From *Total Recall* to *The Thirteenth Floor*, movie directors invite us to see that the context in which we find ourselves might be preventing us from seeing reality as it actually is.

Often enough our society feeds off of others, and we are oblivious to the harms and injustices that it perpetrates. Still, we need to ask ourselves, are we responsible for this? Are we responsible for the fact that the world cannot support the lifestyle that most Americans live: the energy resources, the meat and fish consumption, the use of transportation, and so on?

Thomas Aquinas would simply ask, could we have known otherwise? In each of the movies I mentioned, the heroes are those who find out the truth against all odds. They allow themselves to think outside the box and to wonder whether they really understand what is actually going on. We are required to do the same. And our failure to learn otherwise is a clear indication of how we sin from strength, from a failure to bother to love. In the comfort and luxury of our society, we keep one another from knowing what we need to know, what we could know, and what we do not bother to learn.

Faced with this notion of sin, should we not despair? Should we not give up? Should we just go away sad?

There is that famous parable of the rich young man. In it, he goes up to Jesus and asks what he must do to get into heaven, and Jesus tells him to observe the commandments. The rich young man responds complacently: I did all that. But Jesus says, okay, give up everything and come follow me. And the rich man goes away sad.

When we think that God wants us to love as best we can, inevitably we become like the rich young man, very unwilling to love more than what is comfortable. When we are really honest, at some point we see that we are each the rich young man. None of us could do anything more than the rich young man.[9] We eventually do not bother to love.

What are we to do? That is, of course, the question the disciples ask Jesus when the young man walks away. Then Jesus explains that what is impossible for us is possible for God. Even though the rich young man could not win his salvation, God in Jesus Christ could.

And that is what sin teaches us. When, like the rich man, we get a glimpse of our sinfulness, we have a choice—to go away despairing or to become modest, humble, and grateful for Christ's salvation.

When we choose the latter, when we really get a glimpse of what we could do but do not bother to, we no longer look on the other as worse than we are. We no longer nestle into our complacency; we become instead transformed in humility.

Furthermore, when we see our sinfulness through the salvation won by Christ, we do not become paralyzed by guilt. Rather we become freed from it, but by Christ. And we never dare look back at our sinfulness lest we become like Lot's wife, paralyzed by our own histories of failing to bother to love.

Sin teaches us never to look back complacently but always to look forward in love and in hope. It teaches us that indeed we are strong and capable of much and that much of our history is filled with how we could have loved but did not bother to love. But the history of sin is one that rebukes us into remembering that we do indeed need our Redeemer and Savior. In short, because of sin, we need Christ. Without that knowledge, we fail to recognize that need.

When we recognize that need, we recognize also our neighbor, particularly the alienated and marginalized, those who are overwhelmed by the social structures that harness them but benefit us. And we begin to realize that until we work in solidarity and justice for all, we have not yet accepted the liberating redemption of Jesus Christ.

Grace is not cheap. When we finally understand what it is that Christ has done for us, we inevitably learn to open our eyes and see what we can do. And from that strength, we learn what we need to know and need to do. [10]

STUDY QUESTIONS

1. How do you define sin? What is for you a good example of sin?
2. Why is it important to understand not only that we are called to love, but that we sin? Do you think people are willing to see that they are sinners? Do you think we should just see ourselves as good?
3. Do you think we primarily sin from strength or weakness? Why is it that so many people think that we sin from weakness?
4. What movies can you think of that try to show us that we are indeed living in a self-deceptive world?
5. Are you hope-filled that we can work for a more just world?

Chapter Four

Suffering

When we examine suffering, we need to recognize two very different types of discussion on this topic. The more familiar occurs in academic gatherings, which produce many philosophical and theological works about suffering and its "meaning." The less familiar occurs in those intimate settings in which we are called to respond to someone who is suffering and who wants to talk with us about her or his suffering; in that setting, we usually listen rather than talk.

In the academic context there is less interest in the actual sufferer and more interest in the question of theodicy—that is, how can we reconcile a merciful, providential God with suffering? These academic works are really not addressed to sufferers, but rather to a general audience philosophically or theologically interested in the questions that result from the reality of suffering in a world created by a loving God. These works tend to be theoretical and speculative, rather than practical and concrete.

Another way of describing these two conversations is to note that there is the intellectual level, where we "search for reasons *why* there is suffering in the world and *why* it comes to some and not to others." The other is much less abstract and much more strategic, what some call the survival level, where we "provide support and comfort to the person who is experiencing suffering."[1]

In the latter case, we listen to how the suffering person tries to figure out ways of surviving through their suffering.

As you have probably guessed by now, I am more interested in understanding suffering from the latter viewpoint, the viewpoint of the sufferer. Then we can turn to the question of suffering and its meaning. In all this, we need to learn what our response to suffering ought to be.

VOICE

Faced with suffering, we need to recognize the critical importance of listening. In order to appreciate the importance of listening, however, we must appreciate the importance of the sufferer's voice.

Nowhere has the relationship between the voice and suffering been better captured than by Elaine Scarry. In the first chapter of her book *The Body in Pain*, Scarry studies the relationship between voice and torture. She explains that the object of torture is not to learn information, but rather to force the tortured person to accuse herself and thereby to recognize the torturer's power. Torturers derive their understanding of power from the voices of the tortured. Thus the torturer aims to make tortured persons convict themselves. This happens when the tortured person's body is so broken with pain that she is unable to keep her voice from submitting to the fictive power of the torturer. The aim of torture, then, is to tear the voice from its body, to make the tortured person capitulate to the torturer's authority. Scarry writes, "The goal of the torturer is to make the one, the body, emphatically and crushingly *present* by destroying it, and to make the other, the voice, *absent* by destroying it." At the end of torture, the tortured person is finally left voiceless; once the voice in agony acknowledges the torturer's power, it falls into shameful, isolating silence. [2]

Scarry notes that the tortured person's most difficult wound to heal is also the voice. For this reason, Amnesty International assists the tortured, unable out of shame to tell their narratives, to read and understand their records so that one day they may articulate or give voice to the truth of the atrocities they endured. When they are able to finally speak the truth about the experience of torture, they enter on to the journey of healing, but until they do, they live in silent shame. Scarry's work convincingly demonstrates the centrality of the human voice in attaining healing integration.

Through the voice we express our fundamental concerns, maintain relationships, organize our world, and locate ourselves among others. But when we suffer, our dependence on the voice is itself troublesome particularly because the terrors and trauma associated with the threat and the loss experienced in suffering often inhibit the sufferer from intelligibly articulating the cause and/or depth of suffering. Moreover, the voice itself, not merely the sufferer's intelligence, is also, especially in times of pain, muted. Thus, when the voice is unable to express itself, the sufferer loses the most integral way by which a sufferer can communicate and remain in contact with the community that supports her. Progressively, studies show us not only the therapeutic function that the voice has in the life of the sufferer, but conversely the compounded suffering that occurs when the voice is ignored, lost, or silenced. For, like torture itself, the act of silencing a sufferer, or worse, of making a suffering person speak against herself, is a violent action.

Here I think of not only the tortured but also of the sick, and I think of the many instances when we try to keep those who are sick from telling us how badly they feel. We think in our exercises that we are encouraging the sick to look on the so-called brighter side, when actually we are only telling the patient, "Don't, please don't tell me what you're worrying about. I can't bear to hear it." Of course, the sufferer is the one who has to bear the reality that we only refuse to hear.

I think particularly of those patients—who, facing their own mortality, find that same violence in the habitual acts wherein physicians and nurses as well as family and friends ignore, silence, translate, or belittle the voices of patients. How many times, when a person's death is near, is the only one disposed to speaking about the future the patient, but the discomfort of the others is so great as to inhibit, diminish, or worse, contradict the very person who wants to speak about her forthcoming death.

The sufferer's voice is their lifeline to the world from which they find themselves progressively isolated. Thus, through the voice, the one isolated in suffering is able to reach out to others. For this reason we need to consider not only the voice of the sufferer but also the listening of those who seek to respond to the sufferer.

RESPONDING TO THE SUFFERER BY LISTENING

Listening is all the more important when the sufferer is not immediately forthcoming about her own well-being or about the strategies of her survival. This inability to express easily one's suffering or one's strategies is, in fact, a commonplace, since the act of articulating the perceived threat to one's world is itself traumatic.

In a source that I am unable to remember or locate, I read that in many patient interviews, patients do not name their major ailment until they first mention one or two lesser ones. That is, during an interview, the first two items reported by many patients are not the reasons for the patient's visit, but the third item is—"I haven't slept well. I have an occasional headache, but nothing serious. Oh yes, I have a lump on my breast." We delay the reporting because we have never had to face what we fear facing. Thus, on occasion, the inattentive or rushed physician sends home a patient who never utters the real reason for their concern. (Here is a curious parallel. In my training for hearing confessions, I was informed that it is not until the third sin that penitents express their serious sins. Not uncommonly we hear things like "I swore, I missed mass, I committed adultery, I was testy at work.") Listening requires an active patience, a soliciting ear.

Still, there is something more integral for responding to suffering than simply hearing the correct condition. The act of listening should welcome the sufferer who wants to speak. Allowing the sufferer to speak is a very biblical stance. Here I want us to consider God's listening to the suffering of Job and then the suffering of Jesus.

The book of Job begins with God delighting in his servant Job, an upright man. The devil says to God, if Job was visited with suffering, he wouldn't be all that wonderful. With that, the story unfolds of calamitous actions happening to Job that lead to the loss of his wealth, the deaths of his children, and the covering of his body with pustules. Job wonders, *Why me?* He laments and cries out to God. He hears no answer from God, but is visited by his "friends." Surprisingly, they come and tell him that his suffering is due to his own fault. They claim a person suffers after doing something wrong. Job is responsible, therefore, for his suffering they surmise. Poor Job is not only suffering, but being blamed for it as well.

J. David Pleins asks, where is God in the midst of Job's suffering and complaint? Why does God not respond immediately to Job? Why does God let Job be judged and silenced by his so-called friends? Pleins responds that it is not God's absence but "God's silence [that] dominates the discussions of Job with his friends."[3] Pleins contends that God is the only one who gives Job a hearing, who allows Job to utter his complaint, and who gives Job the time to find a way of articulating his understanding of his situation. God is the one who, by listening, empowers Job's struggle and witnesses Job's integrity. God is the listener to Job. The others interrupt, confound, or silence Job.

This insight about a listening God is applicable to understanding the same "absence" or "silence" of God at Golgotha. We might wonder what those few witnesses thought when, as they stood helpless at the cross of Jesus, they heard Jesus's words, "My God, my God, why have you forsaken me?" (Matt. 27:46). But they listened to the cry of the suffering Jesus. Is God absent or, as Pleins suggests, is God listening? God witnesses to Jesus's agony and does not contend with Jesus's complaint, but he does give Jesus a full hearing. God's silence both in Job and at the crucifixion conveys a God who listens actively, accompanying us in our suffering, allowing and empowering us to speak.

How many times have we acted differently? How many times have we said to one in their suffering, "Oh, don't say that!" "Oh, you don't mean that!" "Oh, but that's not right!" How many times do our standards of etiquette or decorum prompt us to interrupt the one who is lamenting her or his suffering? Against those times, the God of Job and Jesus is still listening to the cry of the sufferer.

This listening stands as an important witness to the sufferer and as a key alternative to another Christian urge, which is to interpret in the face of suffering. A senior colleague with whom I normally agree argues that Christians differentiate suffering from pain precisely in that "pain demands a response, while suffering demands an interpretation." I am not too sure that suffering demands an interpretation because so much suffering is so senseless. If suffering is so senseless, how could it have meaning?

In fact, I think the Christian urge to translate or interpret another's suffering can also be as violent as the act of silencing. I think here specifically of when Catholic leaders known for wanting to better Christian-Jewish relations let their own theology of suffering interpret the Jewish suffering in the Holocaust. Worse still is the insistence of Christians to speak about another's suffering, especially when they were the cause of that suffering. Marcel Sarot brings this point out poignantly in his "Auschwitz, Morality, and the Suffering of God."[4] There Sarot cites numerous instances of Christians translating or interpreting the meaning of Jewish questions and answers in the aftermath of Auschwitz. He especially addresses the Christian insistence to answer the Jewish sufferer who asks, "Where is God in all this?" Indeed, one has to remind the Christian that the Jew might not necessarily be looking for an answer to the question. Sarot calls his fellow Christian theologians to draw a moratorium on raising up Auschwitz as providing testimony necessary to understand faith and suffering, and he contends that the primary question that we Christians should raise in the face of Auschwitz is "How can we prevent that Christianity ever again can provide fertile soil for antisemitism and kindred movements?"

The Christian insistence on interpreting in the face of suffering should give way, I think, to the Jewish insistence on listening. One writer argues that "Christians would do better to face up to the pointlessness [of suffering], taking a lesson from the Hebrew scriptures. The psalms of lament . . . make no attempt to explain or palliate. Instead they give voice to human anguish, rage and despair on the apparent assumption that the God of Israel is strong enough to take it."[5]

Still, the call to listen to the voice of the one who is suffering is not always easy because sometimes the sufferer cannot speak. For instance, often suffering results precisely because a person is in pain and unable to express herself. In some instances this inability to speak is an even greater suffering than the pain itself because the sufferer is acutely aware of her isolation and is unable to communicate it. In particular, the person in chronic pain finds often that the pain perpetually keeps the sufferer from speaking. Pain inhibits the sufferer from doing the only thing that the sufferer wants to do: communicate her pain.

To assist the one suffering we need to remember the empathetic quality of pain that helps us acknowledge the depth of the other's suffering. Through empathy we can develop an aesthetic sense by which we can try to apprize the suffering of another who cannot speak but who communicates her suffering through a variety of movements. This aesthetic sense can be especially developed when the listener is attentive to the nature of suffering in her or his own life. When we become aware of the narrative of pain within our own bodies, we become familiar again with the desire to give voice to our own pain, hopefully assisting us to learn to listen to another's own "silent" narrative of suffering. Revisiting the terrain of one's own past suffering establishes the groundwork for becoming a compassionate and perceptive listener.

That the body can express the depth and complexity of suffering is very important. Where there is no voice to express the suffering, then we are reminded that "the body never lies." Thus, even when the sufferer cannot voice in any way her or his suffering, still the body may be able to communicate its suffering.

Here we can accompany another as we read aloud the psalms of lament as a means by which a listener can enter into solidarity with those who can only groan out or twist and turn in their suffering.[6] With these psalms, the sufferer, unable to express or name the particularity of her suffering, may be able to sense a welcoming acknowledgment by the listener of the desire to communicate to some extent the depth of personal suffering. By reciting the psalms for one unable to speak, we can become the sufferer's surrogate voice.

Still, there may be instances when the sufferer may not want to communicate, may not want yet to share her or his suffering. In fact, not talking might be for some a temporary survival strategy. Here I recall how my niece Megan responded to the awful news that she was out of remission. Because of her cancer she had lost a year of high school, just one year before graduation. In remission she returned to her high school a year later, but now with a different senior class. She made many friends in this new class and was quite happy. She learned about coming out of remission, however, about six weeks before her senior graduation.

The hospital staff wanted to talk about a bone marrow transplant. She informed them that there would be no transplant until she was graduated from high school. There had been enough conversations about the transplant earlier in her cancer, she maintained, and it was already known that her lone sibling was a match and had agreed to be the donor. A day after graduation she would be ready for the transplant, but there would be no discussion before then.

This was an awkward time. When she would come into Boston to treat the occasional infections that she developed during these six weeks, I would sit with her in the hospital. One day I said, "Megan, I don't want to discuss the transplant. I know you don't want any of us to. But could you give me an indication that you know what lays before you?" "I do know," she said.

She knew that she might not survive the transplant, but she also knew that she could celebrate her graduation. She had already lost one graduation due to her first year of treatments and she was not going to lose another graduation. Her graduation was wonderful!

Later, Megan underwent the transplant and all of its "opportunistic" infections. She bore those indignities with the same indomitable spirit as she had the earlier ones. Then, after passing the famed one-hundred-days-after-transplant mark, she and the rest of us began to sigh with relief. Unfortunately, it was only an idle reprieve and at nineteen Megan succumbed to the battle she valiantly fought for three years. Throughout it all, though the cancer had its way, Megan was very much the decision maker, the agent, the person, and her graduation—rightfully—was the centerpiece of her own very human and very true triumph.

Another story involves me. In 1991, my dad died one month after I began teaching at Weston Jesuit School of Theology. It was a very hard time for all of us. Eight months earlier, my parents' home, along with everything that they owned, was destroyed in a fire. They rebuilt the house, sold it, and moved to Florida. They had only just picked out a condo, which was being built when my dad died. After his death I frequently flew to Florida to help my mom, I was dealing with my own grief, and I was trying to figure out how to teach at Weston.

With grief we have our good days and bad days. One day I was having a good one, until a colleague of mine stopped me in the stairwell that leads from the office building's lobby. With people passing all around me she grabbed my hand and asked me, "Jim, how are you?" I said that I was fine. "No, Jim, how are you?" "Fine, thank you," I said, now trying to get away, though she held my hand tighter. "No, Jim, how are you really?" I said, "I'm fine, thank you," and left.

I was angry and hurt. She wanted me to unleash my grief in the lobby before other colleagues, the staff, and my students. And for whose benefit? Sometimes we think the willingness to listen brings with it the right to examine or, in this case, interrogate the sufferer.

Sometimes the sufferer can communicate quite loudly and clearly. They might, in fact, contradict our expectations. Here we may want to remember a claim I made in the chapter on love. There I remarked that whereas we might be called to love Christ in the neighbor, we are first called to love the neighbor as they are in themselves. Nowhere is this more remarkable than in the sufferer who faces their threats in uncannily candid ways.

The womanist theologian M. Shawn Copeland turns to the words of black slave women to see how they responded to the continuous powerful oppression of their "owners." She helps us to hear in the cry of those slave women not necessarily just words of desperation and fear, but also words of resistance, triumph, and, as Copeland puts it, sass. Through voice, sufferers articulate their own rightful resistance to suffering.

Copeland specifically turns to the voices of the black slave singing the spirituals:

The spirituals . . . were an important resource of resistance. . . . The spirituals reshaped and conflated the characters and stories, parables and pericopes, events and miracles of the Hebrew and Christian scriptures. These songs told the mercy of God anew and testified to the ways in which the enslaved people met God at the whipping post, on the auction block, in the hush arbor, in the midnight flight to freedom. . . . If the makers of the spirituals glorified in singing of the cross of Jesus, it was not because they were masochistic and enjoyed suffering. Rather, the enslaved Africans sang because they saw in the rugged wooden planks One who had endured what was their daily portion. The cross was treasured because it enthroned the One who went all the way with them and for them. The enslaved Africans sang because they saw the result of the cross—triumph over the principalities and powers of death, triumph over evil in this world.[7]

In the spirituals we hear voices uttering a language of redemption. But Copeland introduces another way in which black women during slavery voiced their suffering through the language of resistance: "In these narratives, women model audacious behavior: wit, cunning, verbal warfare, and moral courage. These Black women *sass! The Random House Dictionary of the English Language* defines *sass* as 'impudent or disrespectful back talk.' Enslaved black women used sass to guard, regain, and secure self-esteem; to obtain and hold psychological distance; to speak truth; to challenge the atmosphere of moral ambiguity that surrounds them; and sometimes to protect against sexual assault."[8]

Copeland teaches us that if we really want to understand suffering we might want to listen to the experienced, articulate voice of the sufferer. Sometimes we might not hear what we would like. Perhaps we find the spirituals more acceptable than the sass. But if we silence the sass then we are not unlike those whom Scarry writes about, those who try to inhibit the voices of the suffering.

When the sufferer is resistant we hear another language spoken. Copeland elaborates: "A theology of suffering in a womanist perspective is resistant. With motherwit, courage, sometimes their fists and most often sass, Black women resisted the degradation of chattel slavery. . . . With sass, Black women defined themselves and dismantled the images that had been used to control and demean them. With sass, Black women turned back the shame that others tried to put on them. With sass, Black women survived, even triumphed over emotional and psychic assault."[9]

These models remind us again who are the principal agents in suffering: not ourselves nor God, but the sufferers—those who occasionally, in order to lay claim to their own universe, may at times moan, cry, sing, scream, remain silent, or even give us sass. But inevitably, by trying to voice their own concerns, they invite us into the task of seeing the threat to their universe.

Before we turn to the "meaning" of suffering, I offer three narratives about speaking through one's suffering. The first again regards my niece Megan, who suffered a rare strain of leukemia before her death at nineteen. Megan asserted herself quite clearly, especially whenever a physician, seeing her as a child, albeit at sixteen, seventeen, or eighteen years of age with a life-threatening illness, treated her as a child to be seen but not heard. Once a physician had wrongly inserted her port and he was trying to correct it by pressing powerfully against her chest. Megan moaned, cried, and asked him to stop. He ignored her and persisted more aggressively. Finally, she let loose with a string of expletives that stunned us all; my sister, brother-in-law, and I were amazed, though the nurses were elated. This doctor who showed no compassion to children was finally frightened by a child; he tried to intimidate. Unfortunately for Megan, she had to stoop to his depths, but she gave him a lesson that many before her wanted to give him.

The second concerns Connie, a lawyer friend of mine and a devoted mother of three, whose middle daughter, Maureen, was an eleven-year-old fighting leukemia at the same time as Megan. She told me the story of a little eight-year-old in the hospital bed next to her daughter who was also suffering from leukemia. A nurse came in to give the girl an injection and the girl cried, "I'm afraid." "No, you're not afraid; you are a big girl," contradicted the nurse, giving the girl her injection. After the nurse left, my friend Connie went over to the girl's mother and said, "Excuse me, but I would never let a nurse or doctor contradict my child. Things are bad enough that she should have to conform her suffering to the nurse's efficiency."

On another occasion Maureen, suffering from punctured lungs, had been living for several weeks with tubes in her chest. An older woman in her room had a similar catheter. The older woman said to Maureen, "Honey, when they put that thing in your chest did they say that you would experience 'discomfort'?" "Yes," Maureen responded. "You know, discomfort is sitting in a wooden chair for twenty minutes or wearing tight shoes. That thing hanging out of your chest isn't discomfort; it's living hell." Little Maureen facing leukemia found in that woman someone who knew her suffering. But those who translated her suffering as "discomfort" were unable to listen, let alone understand the little girl's living hell.

WHAT IS SUFFERING?

Eric Cassell, author of *The Nature of Suffering*, distinguishes pain from suffering by making the simple observation that pain can exist without suffering and suffering can exist without pain. He describes suffering as "the distress brought about by the actual or perceived impending threat to the integrity or continued existence of the whole person." That is, suffering emerges when people become aware of the fact that something necessary for them is not only beyond their grasp, but also might never again be attainable. Cassell notes, therefore, that suffering arises with "the loss of the ability to pursue purpose."[10] People suffer when they actually lose some good or when they recognize they may never obtain some good that is seriously important for them to have: health, mobility, a loving marriage, a trusted friend, a decent job.

In the actual loss of a good, they recognize that their own well-being and their own general relatedness with others are also diminished. In the case of foreseeing the necessary good as unattainable, they similarly recognize their future well-being and general relatedness as also threatened. Thus, when people suffer, they find themselves marginalized from those who enjoy the very goods they have lost or were hoping would be theirs. They experience a sense of isolation, a sense that they do not have what brings others together. Not only do they feel marginalized by the loss of what was had or what was expected, but the feeling itself occurs individually and privately. Cassell writes, "Suffering is necessarily private because it is ultimately individual."[11]

Human beings are, however, enormously resourceful. When they find themselves isolated and at a loss, they develop "a drive to survive." Within that drive, they develop strategies that they pursue as goals that are alternatives to the goods and the type of relatedness that will not be theirs. Moreover, the sufferer pursues a survival strategy in which their present relationships are adapted according to whether the others—family, friends, neighbors—support them in the survival strategies.

We need therefore to appreciate that when people suffer they have four defining experiences: first, they find that they are without something necessary for their incorporation with the rest of humanity; second, their personal feeling, experience, or sense of loss heightens their perceived isolation from others; third, they search for a way to renegotiate the future of their lives so that they can recoup whatever humanity was lost in the first place; and fourth, they look to their many relationships to see who will support them on their search. On this final note, we can think of the many support groups that arise for all sorts of people who have experienced loss. People who suffer often turn to these groups to help them deal with these four experiences that accompany suffering.

RELIGIOUS RESPONSES TO SUFFERING

In his famous book *Christ*, the great Dominican theologian Edward Schillebeeckx (1914–2009) describes how different cultures address the question of suffering. Regarding religious societies, he remarks that while each religion has a different specific response to one who suffers, they share "the fact that they give the last word to the *good*, and not to evil and suffering . . . their deepest concern is to overcome suffering."[12]

Commenting on the Jews, Schillebeeckx remarks that, in the Bible, "Israel has no problems with suffering which men bring upon themselves through their own sinfulness." But Israel "protests and guards itself against unmerited suffering." Apart from sinfulness, Israel "did not simply want to accept suffering as a *given*."[13]

We need to appreciate that, regarding sin and suffering, Israel did not believe that suffering was a punishment from God for sin. Rather, Israel believed that suffering is the natural consequence of sin: if by sin one departs from the providential way of the Lord God, one will in all likelihood get lost, run into trouble, and eventually experience hardships. The notion that God punishes the sinner is a deeply questionable Christian invention. In fact, it would seem to me that this Jewish insight of suffering as at times a natural consequence of sin is a far better way of explaining why we often experience suffering in light of sin. Attributing suffering to a "punishing" God is quite absurd, no?

Still, Israel recognizes that some suffering occurs that is not as a result of sin. In fact, Israel experiences such suffering. Schillebeeckx remarks that because of belief in God, "Israel did not hesitate to direct hard questions to God. 'Is God asleep?' asks Ps. 44:23, 26."[14] Therefore, until God delivers Israel from suffering, Israel protests over God's delay.

Christians also see God and suffering as "diametrically opposed; where God appears, evil and suffering have to yield. So there is no place for suffering." Moreover, Schillebeeckx remarks that, unlike Job's friends, Jesus "breaks with the idea that suffering necessarily has something to do with sinfulness." Looking at the description of the man born blind in John's Gospel (John 9:2f.) and the account of the murdered Galileans in Luke's Gospel (Luke 13:1–5), we see "that it is possible to draw conclusions from sin to suffering, but not from suffering to sin." That is, we cannot assume that one's suffering is due to one's sinfulness.

Schillebeeckx then turns to the Christian notion of redemptive suffering and again dismisses the notion of a Christian God who sends suffering our way. Schillebeeckx provides strong testimony regarding Christian faith and suffering that in some circles is often misunderstood. Though he acknowledges that some suffering may actually help some individuals to become more sensitive and compassionate and, in some instances, actually transform a person, still he says decisively, "there is an excess of suffering and evil in our history."

I find Schillebeeckx here very helpful. I can see someone in their own suffering trying to see its meaning in their lives, and they may at some point say that the suffering has helped them, that it is redemptive. But I find it difficult to ascribe it to another's suffering. For instance, like others, I have met parents suffering over the death of a child, migrant workers unable to care adequately for their children, the people at Smokey Mountain in the Philippines, where tens of thousands literally live in a garbage dump. I have sat with people in terrible suffering from cancer or HIV/AIDS. I have read about survivors of families swept away by mudslides from typhoons, taken away in tornadoes in the Midwest or by hurricanes in the South. I have heard about earthquakes in already devastated parts of the world, floods and famine affecting people barely able to survive, refugees adrift at sea. I can think of the victims of war in Rwanda, Nigeria, Poland, Germany, the Philippines. I cannot understand why they have that suffering. I cannot call this suffering redemptive. Rather, I am struck silent.

Schillebeeckx confirms our experiences as he continues: "There is a barbarous excess, for all the explanations and interpretations. There is too much *unmerited* and *senseless* suffering for us to be able to give an ethical, hermeneutical and ontological analysis of our disaster." He surmises, "human reason cannot in fact cope with concentrated historical suffering and evil."[15] But he adds that not only human reason, but the scriptures too cannot explain away suffering. He writes:

> The Christian message does not give an *explanation* of evil or our history of suffering. That must be made clear from the start. Even for Christians, suffering remains impenetrable and incomprehensible, and provokes rebellion. Nor will the Christian blasphemously claim that God himself required the death of Jesus as compensation for what *we* make of our history.[16]

Schillebeeckx offers us, however, another way of looking at redemptive suffering and that is by giving it an ultimately liberating significance. This is the suffering that persons assume in their responsible concern to overcome others' greater suffering. Here is love electing suffering to help another, and the primary model for this love is God.

On this point, the wonderful late Presbyterian theologian William Placher (1948–2008) describes eloquently the suffering of God:

> God suffers because God is vulnerable, and God is vulnerable because God loves—and it is love, not suffering or even vulnerability, that is finally the point. . . . The freedom of love is good, and that freedom risks suffering and, in a sinful world full of violence and injustice, will always encounter it sooner or later. Love does not regret the price it pays for making itself vulnerable, but to speak of paying a price is itself to acknowledge that the suffering is itself an evil. Vulnerability, on the other hand, is a perfection of loving freedom.[17]

We imitate God when we practice this vulnerability and its accompanying mercy—that is, the willingness to enter into the chaos of another. That merciful act often entails an elective suffering for the sake of others.

Here another Dominican, Sister Mary Catherine Hilkert, discusses the importance of solidarity with those who suffer by reflecting on the lives of the four American church women (Maura Clarke, Ita Ford, Dorothy Kazel, and Jean Donovan) who were killed in December 1980 in El Salvador. There we see the nature of one's commitment to stand in solidarity with those who suffer. We can find in these four women's testimonies how, when, and why embracing the suffering of another is an imitation of Christ, an act of vulnerable love. Hilkert writes, "These women embraced solidarity with the poor not out of any glorification or romanticization of suffering, but because it was among the poor of the world that they discovered the good news of the reign of God at work in the world despite all evidence to the contrary."[18]

Hilkert invites us to listen to these women's decisions to stand in solidarity with those who suffer. Ita Ford wrote of her decision to enter into Christ's own paschal mystery, the mystery of suffering, death, and resurrection: "Am I willing to suffer with the people here, the suffering of the powerless? Can I say to my neighbors, 'I have no solution to this situation; I don't know the answers, but I will walk with you, search with you, be with you?'"[19]

Two weeks before her death, Jean Donovan asked about how her own self was being stretched by the decision to stay in solidarity with those whom she served: "Several times I have decided to leave El Salvador. I almost could except for the children, the poor, the bruised victims of this insanity. Who would care for them? Whose heart could be as staunch as to favor the reasonable thing in a sea of their tears and loneliness? Not mine, dear friend, not mine."[20] The decision of these brave women who were brutally murdered on December 2, 1980, stands as a clear example of vulnerable love or redemptive suffering.

Reading Schillebeeckx on suffering is very helpful. He notes what all religions have in common: the religious response to suffering is to find a way of eliminating suffering. Moreover, he corrects those false impressions of Christianity (which too often Christians promote) that seem to make suffering an expression of a loving God's will, and he offers us a palpable notion of redemptive suffering but in the key of solidarity, mercy, and liberation.

But I think he leaves us short on one particular point: he trusts too much in the distinction between "merited" and "unmerited" suffering. Schillebeeckx acknowledges that the book of Job, like the Gospels of Luke and John, debunks any attempt to suggest that where there is suffering there must have been sin. Nonetheless, Schillebeeckx leaves unacknowledged the problem of the distinction between "merited" and "unmerited" suffering.

To the extent that we maintain this distinction, we believe that we can discern whose suffering is merited and whose is not. To the extent that we leave the distinction intact, we still believe that we can determine who should be beneficiaries of our compassion and who should not. But how can we know that someone's suffering is really "unmerited"? How do we arrive at such divine judgment? Does the AIDS victim have to be a child or a hemophiliac? Does the cancer victim really have to have been taking every precaution against carcinogens? Does the tortured political activist really have to have been politically prudent? Does the date-rape victim really have to be insisting "No" the entire evening?

The distinction between merited and unmerited suffering strikes me as still engaging the albeit-modified stance of the so-called friends of Job—Eliphaz, Bildad, and Zophar—who contended with Job about his "merited suffering." My point is, if we believers only stand in protest against unmerited suffering, how are we to know what is and what is not merited? And if we insist on the distinction, it seems to me that a deep residue of moralism is apparent wherever listeners are encouraged to sift out the "merited" from "unmerited" sufferers.

For instance, have you not attended a wake and heard people whisper right by the casket: "He should have quit smoking earlier." "She should have left him years ago." "He should have gone on that diet." "She never took care of herself." Why do we make these utterances? For whose benefit do we make them? The poor person is already dead! We are standing right there over the casket, purportedly "paying our respects," and somehow we righteously decide that we need to blame the deceased for their death. Why is it that whenever anyone dies, it is invariably their fault? "I told him he shouldn't drive that car." "If she stayed home more often, she wouldn't have been on that plane." "He should never have walked home that way." "I always have thought that microwave ovens are dangerous!"

Let us not deny that evidently some suffering is tragically unmerited, but I am sure that in many instances we have a propensity to judge another's suffering as merited. Is not the ultimate purpose of this dubious distinction to winnow out those people whom we believe are not worthy of our compassion? And are we not far harsher in our judgment than our all-seeing God is? So are we not finally left with the distinction as little more than a device that allows us to withdraw compassion and to confirm our self-serving righteousness? The distinction allows us, I think, the opportunity to parse out our sympathy in very condescending and stingy ways.

STUDY QUESTIONS

1. How do you define suffering?
2. From what experiences of yours, with family and friends, did you come to understand suffering better?
3. If God is all loving, why do people suffer?
4. Do you think that a person's ability to express their suffering is necessary for healing?

Part II

The Texts

Chapter Five

The Ten Commandments

In the following section, I address three questions: How did the Ten Commandments enter into the tradition of moral wisdom? How were they used? And how can they be used today?

THE TEN COMMANDMENTS AND THE TRADITION OF MORAL THEOLOGY

From the sixth to the sixteenth century almost all of moral theology aimed to assist priests in the proper administration of the sacrament of penance. Before Pope Innocent III levied the Easter duty, mostly monks, nuns, and nobility confessed their sins; with the Easter duty, everyone did, at least annually. The texts provided to confessors organized all the sins under the rubric of the so-called seven deadly sins: lust, pride, gluttony, sloth, envy, anger, avarice.

Before the Reformation in the sixteenth century, a number of theologians began to question the privileged position of the seven deadly sins. One key figure is John Gerson (1363–1429), who wanted to provide a more positive, scripture-based formation to Christians and to overcome the minimalist claims of simply avoiding sin. Gerson turned to the Ten Commandments, which he called "the rock of Christian Ethics." His main context for the instruction on the Ten Commandments was a "catechism," and he and others began putting together these accessible, yet somewhat comprehensive, books of Christian instruction.

A century later, during the Reformation, Martin Luther (1483–1546) and John Calvin (1509–1564), and then the fathers of the Council of Trent (1545–1547, 1551–1552, 1562–1563) used the Ten Commandments as the basis of moral instruction in the context of catechetical instruction. Their appeal to the Ten Commandments was itself a repudiation of the primacy accorded to the seven deadly sins, and this for several reasons. First, because they were in the scriptures, the commandments enjoyed the biblical warrant of expressing God's will. Second, unlike the seven deadly sins, they offered not only negative prohibitions but, on occasion, positive prescriptions. Not only do they prohibit killing and stealing, but they imposed on us the duty to honor God, God's name, the Sabbath, and our parents. Finally, with the possible exception of pride, the deadly sins were primarily offensive to human life alone. The commandments, however, specified prescriptions and prohibitions that begin with our relationship with God and moved from there to our relationships with one another.

It is helpful to see an example of how the commandments were used. Martin Luther's *Large Catechism* (1529) dedicated nearly half of its 120 pages to the Ten Commandments. Generally speaking in terms of prohibitions or prescriptions, Luther began his instruction of each commandment by following the specific form of the commandment, but then turned to its corollary. If the commandment was a prohibition, he treated the prohibition first, but then considered its prescriptive features. The fifth commandment on killing began, for instance, with an explanation of the prohibition, but turned eventually to consider the failure to do good to one's neighbor: "God rightly calls all persons murderers who do not offer counsel and aid to men in need and in peril of body and life."

Furthermore, Luther's explanations focused not on particular external actions that were in themselves right or wrong, but rather on interior dispositions and particular relationships. That is, more than focusing on particular actions that were outlawed, Luther considered the vices that gave birth to some actions.

Finally, the heart dominated Luther's interpretation of the commandments. He concludes the first commandment: "Where the heart is right with God and this commandment is kept, fulfillment of all the others will follow of its own accord."

These three features—matching prohibition and prescription; emphasizing habitual, relational conduct; and acting always from a charitable heart—became the fundamental format for instructing on the Ten Commandments. Moreover, Roman Catholics as well as the followers of Martin Luther and John Calvin recognized in the Ten Commandments a moral foundation that was biblically based, had both prescriptions and prohibitions, asserted the priority of the interior disposition over the exterior action, and began with our relationship with God and moved to our relationship with one another. Indeed, the Ten Commandments were recognized again as "the rock of Christian Ethics."

Here they are as taught by the Catholic Church today:

1. I am the Lord your God, you shall not have strange gods before me.

2. You shall not take the name of the Lord your God in vain.
3. Remember to keep holy the Lord's Day.
4. Honor your father and your mother.
5. You shall not kill.
6. You shall not commit adultery.
7. You shall not steal.
8. You shall not bear false witness against your neighbor.
9. You shall not covet your neighbor's wife.
10. You shall not covet your neighbor's goods.

HOW WERE THE TEN COMMANDMENTS USED?

After the Reformation, Catholics incorporated the Ten Commandments not only into their catechisms but also into their new moral manuals. Indeed, if the twelfth century marks a break with the penitentials, the sixteenth century marks a break with the confessional manuals.

After the Council of Trent, seminaries were established that required, among other innovations, the formal study of moral theology. With these courses came the need for textbooks, and as a result the moral manuals were developed from the sixteenth to the twentieth century. Of course, like their forerunners, these manuals remain singularly concerned with sin. But now the moral manuals use the Ten Commandments to analyze contemporary cases. What did these moral manuals look like?

One of the first Jesuit moral manuals was by Francisco de Toledo (1532–1596).[1] In 1569, Toledo was made preacher of the papal court and, then, theologian of the Sacred Penitentiary and the Roman Inquisition, as well as counsel to several Roman congregations. In time, he served seven popes. He was made cardinal in 1593, the first Jesuit to receive that honor.[2]

Toledo developed his manual from courses he taught in Rome, but it was not published until two years after his death. Once it was, it was a publishing sensation: it went through seventy-two editions and multitudinous translations, remaining in print until 1716.[3]

We might be a bit surprised at Toledo's treatment of the commandments themselves. In simply counting the number of pages dedicated to the specific commandments, the seventh commandment was by far the most important. While nineteen pages were devoted to the fifth commandment on killing, eighteen to the fourth on honoring parents, and a mere twelve to the sixth commandment on sex, eighty-eight pages were dedicated to the seventh commandment. Similarly, the eighth commandment consisted of thirty-one pages and the ninth (today's tenth) commandment, a surprising thirty-five pages. His evident disinterest with sexual matters was reiterated as he dismissed the matter of the tenth (today's ninth) commandment by simply stating that it was treated under the sixth.[4]

His treatment of the seventh to the ninth commandments concerned social conduct. Rather than being about simple personal or even private acts of theft, lying, or concupiscence, their subject matter was about the structures of relationships in civil and ecclesiastical societies. For the seventh commandment, he examined the fundamental structures of financial institutions. After an introduction, he spent eleven chapters (17–27) on restitution—that is, the social repair of an act of theft. Then he turned to outright money lending or usury,[5] and after four chapters (28–31) on it, he discussed mutual compensation (*lucrum in mutuo*) for loans in three chapters (32–34), restitution of gains accrued from usury in three chapters (35–37), and the innovative public pawn shops turned Franciscan commercial banks (*de monte Pietatis*) in four chapters (38–41). His longest section (42–49) was dedicated to annuities (*census*), and he concluded his comments (50–55) on the seventh commandment on credit agencies (*cambium*).

After these chapters, the eighth commandment focused on the duties in a court of law. A chapter was dedicated to each of the different functionaries in the court: the accused, the state, witnesses, advocates, notaries, and procurators. The final chapters were about what would constitute differences between lies and detraction.

Though he described the ninth commandment as about the social impact of avarice,[6] actually it was about the financial responsibilities of the bishops and clergy. After extensive comments (72–75) on stipends, he turned to six chapters (76–81) on benefices. He concluded the fifth book with two chapters (82–83) on pensions and ten (84–93) on simony—that is, the buying and selling of spiritual benefits.

In examining the actual contents of Toledo's manual, we find none of the traits of the later moral manuals of the nineteenth and twentieth centuries that implicitly depicted, as John Mahoney claimed in his *The Making of Moral Theology*, highly individualistic Roman Catholic penitents obsessed with the law and worried over moral lapses, especially regarding sexual activity. A crippling narcissistic anxiety ran through those pages, which spend their time parsing dubious, scrupulous, and uncertain consciences that were more worried about their private activities than the needs of their neighbor. In Toledo's manual, we find instead a robust social consciousness, a clergy interested in understanding the relevant circumstances of human activity, and a church much more concerned with ascertaining the legitimacy of social practices within existing civil and ecclesial institutions. It might be worth our consideration today.

USING THE TEN COMMANDMENTS TODAY

In this chapter and the next we will look at the two major moral texts in the scriptures: the Ten Commandments and the Beatitudes. In his major work on the two texts, *The Ten Commandments and the Beatitudes: Biblical Studies and Ethics for Real Life*, Lúcás Chan (1968–2015) proposes the texts as the "two moral pillars of the bible" and echoes Raymond Brown when he writes, "The Decalogue expresses God's will, while the Beatitudes reveals the values Jesus prioritized." Lúcás Chan adds that just as "Moses is the conveyer of the Law, the Matthean Jesus is the new lawgiver who calls for a deeper observance of the law and thus is more authoritarian than Moses."[7] Here he reminds us too that in his encyclical *Veritatis Splendor*, Pope John Paul II insisted on the interconnectedness of the two biblical texts.[8] Finally, the Pontifical Biblical Commission saw the two texts as the basic texts to work with in their document *The Bible and Morality: Biblical Roots of Christian Conduct*.[9]

In an earlier work, on the historical study of the emergence of biblical ethics in the Catholic Church, Lúcás Chan argued that the newly emerged field of Catholic biblical ethics needed to be mindful of a double competency needed to do such ethics. First, one needs to know what the specific biblical text meant—that is, one needed the training of a biblicist. Second, one needs to know how we should be ethically formed by the text, and this is what the ethicist provides.[10] Moreover, along with William Spohn, Daniel Harrington, and myself, Lúcás argues that inevitably any application of biblical texts to the moral life can be mediated through the virtues. For all of us, contemporary virtue ethics is a worthy interpreter of contemporary biblical ethics.[11]

Here as we look at three commandments from Exodus 20:2–17, we will follow Lúcás's instruction, learning first what the commandments mean and proclaim, what they summon from us today, and how particular virtues help us to realize those summons.

The Third Commandment, Exodus 20:8–11

Remember the Sabbath day, and keep it holy. For six days you shall labor and do all your work. But the seventh day is a Sabbath to the Lord your God; you shall not do any work—you, your son or your daughter, your male or female slave, your livestock, or the alien resident in your towns. For in six days the Lord made heaven and earth, the sea, and all that is in them, but rested the seventh day; therefore the Lord blessed the Sabbath day and consecrated it.

While noting that after the first, this is the longest commandment, Lúcás notes it is also the only commandment that has both a positive prescription—keep the Sabbath Day holy—and a negative prohibition—you shall not do any work. He also notes that the word *remember* connotes the fact that the practice of rest and worship on the Sabbath seems to have been a long-standing practice, defining Israel. Furthermore the injunction to keep it holy suggests a setting apart of the commandment, therefore dedicating it to the Lord, through a communal worship. In a manner of speaking, the act of keeping the Sabbath holy gives Israel its identity. Nonetheless, since there is no set of practices for keeping it holy, Lúcás suggests with other biblical theologians that the notion of keeping it holy is an interior attitude of reverencing of the day.

Lúcás summarizes lessons learned from the study of the text. First, rest becomes as important and as sacred as work itself, relativizing any tendency of slavery to work. In its call for communal celebration it goes beyond rest. Inasmuch as the imitation of God happens in six days of work, Israel imitates God on the Sabbath. Finally, by banning all work on the Sabbath, all are invited into the celebration of rest.[12]

Christians took from this commandment a key understanding of how this applied to the celebration of Easter.[13] The early Christians did *not* rest on Saturday—the Sabbath—because they were distinguishing themselves from the Jewish people. But they also did not rest on Sunday. On the contrary, lest they be understood as idle members of the Roman Empire, they worked as everyone else did on Sunday.

Still, in the first centuries, the Church Fathers encouraged participation in the Eucharist and the divine office without invoking the third commandment. In fact, the commandment and Sunday worship were not originally considered a perfect match. Sabbath observance was a command to imitate God, the Creator who rested on the Sabbath; Sunday observance was a celebration of Jesus's death, resurrection, and glory.

While the early church resisted Sabbath observance, the emperor Constantine imposed Sunday observance by calling for a cessation of all forms of work, except farming. Then, in the sixth century, the Council of Orleans (538) and later Martin of Braga (d. 580) articulated a prohibition against "servile work." This law was not an imposition or a burden on the serfs themselves; they welcomed the rest and the call to celebrate and to participate in the Christian community. This law was, instead, an imposition on those who owned and controlled the serfs; they now had to let their serfs rest, celebrate the Lord's day, and be gathered into the same faith community of which they were members. The move was extraordinary, for the most marginalized were now incorporated into the community and were also educated by the scriptures. They now belonged to a community in which they previously had not been free enough to participate. The "obligation" then was a liberating one: Sunday observance signified their freedom. Tangibly, Sunday was a foretaste of the promised freedom of the Lord, who has already freed all of us from sin and death.

Centuries later we would forget all this, particularly why "servile work" was originally prohibited. Instead, we developed all sorts of arguments for distinguishing servile work from other forms of permitted work. Servile work no longer meant the work of the serf; it simply meant menial work that should not be done.

The third commandment, as it was originally applied in the church, was a call to be hospitable. In summoning us to observe the Lord's day, it challenges us to participate in the very nature of God as the Creator who rests, the Redeemer who celebrates, and the Sanctifier who gathers. In that triune action we are no longer passive recipients of God's grace, but rather active participants in the Lord's nature, *keeping* the Lord's day holy for all who call upon the name of the Lord.

As the church once had the vision to assure the serfs a place in the church, we have no less a charge today to make the church a place where others encounter a welcome and a dignity not found elsewhere. What would our church look like if it were to welcome *all* people to its table? How would it look were we to actively and regularly welcome people who are poor or emotionally and mentally fragile; women who have had abortions; gays and lesbians who are in loving, committed relationships; divorced but remarried persons struggling for their second or third time in marriage? I am not speaking here about changing church teaching; I'm referring instead to how we can and, I think, should welcome all people, especially to worship.

Or what about our attention to those of other races? A colleague of mine, Father Bryan Massingale, recently tried to find out what Roman Catholic moral theologians had to say about racism during the civil rights movement in the 1960s and 1970s. Massingale found only one reference.[14] Though it is hard to imagine what could be worse than the fact that there was no discussion during the first twenty years of the civil rights movement by Catholic moralists, still the one reference bears examination. It was in answer to the question of whether an African American, who tried to attend mass at his own parish church but found himself barred from entering it because of his race, was still obliged to find a church elsewhere to fulfill his obligation. The moral theologians, both Jesuits, never commented on the racist parish. That entry was the only acknowledgment of racial struggles, a clear indication of how much we have forgotten the original application of the third commandment.

The Fourth Commandment, Exodus 20:12

Honor your father and your mother, so that your days may be long in the land that the Lord your God is giving you.

With regard to the fourth commandment Lúcás Chan points out a debate among scripture scholars as to whether this is the last of the first table or the first of the second. On the one hand, it is the last of the commands that specifically mentions the work of God and is cast, like the first three, in positive terms. But it does point toward honoring others, not God. For this reason, Lúcás sees it as a bridge commandment between the two tables.

Lúcás highlights that "honor" is a fairly all-embracing term that includes obedience but also attitudes and practices of reverence, esteem, and respect. Moreover, like other biblical theologians, he sees that the commandment is aimed at adult children whose days will become long if they honor their parents. This implies that their parents are aged or elderly. Nonetheless, the command is aimed at all children to honor their parents. Additionally, Lúcás notes that mothers and fathers are treated equally and that no one is excluded from this practice that again distinguishes Israel. The injunction to honor is so strong that repeatedly in the Hebrew Bible we find those excoriated who neglect their elderly.[15]

It should not be lost on the reader, I hope, that Lúcás Chan was Chinese and therefore the principle of filial piety is a strong identifying trademark of all in the Confucian tradition. He highlights what those who heed the fourth commandment might learn from filial piety: not only to esteem our parents but also "to maintain attentiveness toward parents and solidarity with them and their feelings and emotions (4:21), to meet them with eagerness and joy (2:8), to offer them readiness and availability (2:6, 4:19), and to exercise gentleness and patience with them (4:19)." He concludes that filial piety extends beyond the parents' deaths.[16]

In this light it might be surprising to consider that if one asked someone today what the fourth commandment means, they will say: "Obey your parents." Peculiar, no? The commandment says "honor your parents," but we translate it as "obey your parents."

We think the fourth commandment calls us to obey because we learned it that way. The first virtue we were taught was the virtue of obedience. It is the virtue that parents, teachers, and babysitters dream and hope every child acquires. Obedience makes a child easier to teach and so the lesson of obedience precedes all others.

By the time we get to the lesson of the Ten Commandments, we have already learned the fourth, but we learn it as "obey." I am not complaining that early in life we learn a corruption of the fourth commandment. That obedience lesson is an important one and because of it we learn many others. Today, however, especially because we live longer, we should return to the original language of honor.

Until recently, we did not think it ordinary for a family to survive three generations. Now we are moving toward the expectation of at least four generations, if not five. Whereas before children did not even meet their grandparents, now they know their great-grandparents. Now sons and daughters know their parents not only for twenty or thirty years, but fifty or sixty years. Whereas before people knew their parents up until the beginning of their own adulthood and were obedient to them, now we know our parents for decades longer and need to honor them.

Honor is a very adult virtue. I learned about honor from my dad. I have to tell you that neither parent was terribly keen on me (the firstborn) leaving home at seventeen to enter the Jesuits. But eventually we all got used to it.

When I was ordained twelve years later, I worked for two successive summers at St. Francis Xavier Church in downtown Manhattan. Every Sunday my dad would make an hour-long drive from Long Island to hear me preach. Later, when I taught at Fordham, he journeyed to the university church whenever I preached, and when I took a parish call on Long Island, he came there, too. He did not come to give me extra support or to teach me anything. He came to listen to me, to honor me. It was then that I learned to honor someone by listening to them.

My dad and I had a wonderful relationship, but it was not until his last years that I learned to honor him. A year before he died at the age of sixty-two, he had open-heart surgery. It was at that time that I considered his mortality, and it was frightening. I told my spiritual director, who in turn gave me great advice: "Talk with your dad, listen to his stories, learn more about him; you don't know how long you have him."

I learned new stories not only about his work, but also about him. On occasion I would ask him what his family was like. I knew his mom, but his dad died before I was born. He would tell me stories of his mom's anxieties and the difficulties they caused him and his sister. He would tell me how poor he and my mom were in their early years of marriage and how they looked for a variety of jobs to supplement his income.

After my dad died, my mom began telling me her stories. She talks about the way she changed high schools, the jobs she had and the better ones she found, and her ambitions and desires to move about. She tells me how she loved working at St. Francis College, how she and my dad met, how they dated, and how he took piano lessons (this stunned me). She talks about death: her dad's during her childhood, her son's (my brother's), her husband's (my dad's), and now her granddaughter's (my niece's).

Her stories were filled with details, more than my dad ever provided. They were above all touching, wonderfully ordinary narratives that told me more about her than any impressions I ever had. These stories had been alive in her memory and now are in my own as well.

I know now how little I really knew my folks. I realize now that all the categories that I created to understand my parents were nothing more than the deep and lasting impressions of a child. I thought I knew them, but I only knew them through the filtered experiences of a child's mind. Even in my adult years I kept seeing their actions as extensions of those same old categories in which I so astutely placed my parents. Now I realize that the only way

I can know who they are is by listening to them, by no longer presuming that I really know them so well, and by willingly asking them to tell me about themselves.

The fourth commandment is not only for my parents' sake. It is, as Lúcás points out, for my sake as well. When we understand that we are called to honor our parents, no matter how old they are or how old we are, we understand once again how much sustained reflection on the commandments brings us in touch with God's will, which is clearly for our benefit. Heeding the commandments leads us not to a burdened life but to our destiny of well-being in love.

The Fifth Commandment, Exodus 20:13

You shall not murder [kill].

Lúcás Chan explains that this is the first of the commandments among equals, but that it depends on the previous commandment: "Life is given to us by God through our parents and hence belongs to God and God alone." But, Lúcás adds, "The protection of human life is the starting point of moving out into the realm of life with others."[17]

Several issues are difficult to understand, however. First, the Hebrew word *ratsach* is often used, though not exclusively, for unauthorized, wrongful, intentional killing—that is, murder. However, it is also used for unintentional killing, in fact, killing without hatred, though still a killing one might be responsible for, as through neglect or manslaughter. Following other scholars, Lúcás argues that the more inclusive form of the word ought to be understood and that therefore, one must always work to protect human life, so that human life is not harmed. Thus Deuteronomy 22:8 mandates the building of a parapet on the roof to prevent the accidental fall of anyone, which could lead to death.

Further, along with other scholars, Lúcás notes that the command finds its real sources in Genesis 9:6, that we are created in God's image and that therefore the taking of human life is a violation of God's creation and dominion. To not exercise the virtue of respect for human life is to not respect the dominion of God. Thus anyone who intentionally takes the life of another is to be put to death (Num. 35:31) for violating God's dominion, a violation for which no atonement or ransom is allowed.

Still, as Lúcás acknowledges, that sanction, the death penalty, as well as the authorized call to war, means that taking human life in these instances is allowed. Here then we can see how socially significant the commandment is. The taking of human life is never a personal right; it can only be a social responsibility as in war or, in former days, a state execution. This needs then to be undergirded by a culture that upholds respect for human life as way of respecting God, our creator who made us in the image of God. There is in this commandment a sacral quality that we must not miss and that needs to be cultivated interiorly throughout all of society.[18]

The command to not kill therefore creates in human society a virtuous respect for the God-givenness of the dignity of human life. It helps us to see that the fabric of society is, in many ways, held together by these commandments that bind us to God and to one another.

Lúcás helps us to see in a study of what the text actually proclaims the immediate impact that the law has on us in all our relatedness. Though the commandments aim to cultivate in us internal attitudes, they have no private purpose, but rather they shape our attitudes with regard to our relatedness to God and with one another. In other words, they undergird the social society and they do so for Israel and for us, both yesterday and today.

STUDY QUESTIONS

1. How did you learn the Ten Commandments?
2. Do you find it helpful to know what the commandment actually means?
3. Do you think that we should worship God on Sunday, or do you think it's up to the person to decide one way or another? In other words, do you believe that there is a commandment to honor God on the Lord's day? Or is it simply a personal choice?
4. Do you think your life is better if you honor your parents? Why?
5. Which commandment do you find to be the most important?
6. Which commandment(s) are the hardest to follow?
7. Do you think that other people in your generation know the Ten Commandments? If they do know them, could they name them?

Chapter Six

Jesus in the New Testament

Before we examine Jesus and God's word, let us reflect on how we think about God.

I would like to try an exercise with you. Think for a moment, what is your image of God? When you pray, when you dwell on God, who is God? Have you a picture, an idea, an image?

I asked that question in 1985 of a very active international community of religious women living and working in Rome. In the community there were about twelve sisters. As the occasional chaplain for the sisters, I was invited one time to lead a day of recollection, and I began the day by asking them to share what their image of God was. I volunteered that my image was the father of the prodigal son. The principal of the school said that she always prayed to Jesus the Teacher. Another, a very charismatic woman, talked about her relationship with the Spirit. One who worked with the infirm saw God as healer, whereas another, probably the freest of us all, saw God as God.

These images are terrific—they help us approach God in prayer and in hope. The image welcomes us and, in many instances, our particular image of God helps us get closer to God. Moreover, as we get older the images of God that most affect us are those that resonate with our particular vocation. Not surprisingly, teachers see Jesus as teacher, and physicians see Jesus as healer.

But these images are also very limiting. I would go to prayer and the Father of the prodigal son could not be nicer. He was always glad to see me! I could go to prayer completely undisturbed. But the God who judges, the God who commands, and the God who is sovereign were nowhere near my image of God. I only saw a nice, rich, fatherly God who hugged me and welcomed me. Like those images of the smiling, good-looking Jesus, how could anyone fail to want to hang out with the father of the prodigal son? Why wouldn't we love just going to sit in prayer with him who will do everything for us?

In order to think rightly about God, then, we need to do three basic things. First, following the first commandment, we must recognize God's sovereignty. This means that as much as we would like to know God, God is also so great that we cannot simply reduce God to an image. Remember Moses and the burning bush? When Moses asked God what God's name was, God resisted Moses's question and answered, "I am who I am." God is not going to let us simply make him into a cool idol. The sovereignty of God lets God be God.

We have to understand that the Creator, Redeemer, and Sanctifier is someone completely beyond us. God eludes us.

Second, we also need to recognize that, because God is love, we are called into an intimate relationship with God, and to do that, we need images that allow us to receive through a mediating way the love of our sovereign God. We need then to constantly allow God's personal but sovereign (or sovereign but personal) love to enter into our lives through mediating images. In order to pray to God, we need the image of God as teacher, father of the prodigal son, as spirit, and so on, but we need to make sure that our image of God is not simply one image. We need to allow other images into our prayer; otherwise we confine our understanding of God to a minimalist understanding.

Third, as we get older, we should look for images that are competitive with one another. The meek and welcoming Jesus who says "Let the children come to me" is different from the angry, principled, righteous person who turns over the tables of the money changers in the Temple. We should literally look to broaden our understanding of God.

In light of the needed tension to let God be God but to let God enter into our lives through images, let us see how the Gospels instruct us.

THE JESUS OF HISTORY AND THE CHRIST OF FAITH

In theology we tend to distinguish our understanding of Jesus into two categories: his life up to and including his death, and his life in glory after his resurrection. We name these categories Jesus of history and the Christ of faith; these are two ways that we know Jesus Christ. The Jesus of history is the Jesus of the Gospels. The Christ of faith is the Lord in glory. However, we will not understand one without the other: if we do not understand the Jesus of history, we will never understand the Christ of faith.

One theologian writes that the scriptures exist to help us get the identity of Jesus right. This is not just a cognitional exercise or, as others would say, a head trip. Rather, we can only get the identity of Jesus right if we surrender all our safe presuppositions about Jesus and if we let Jesus just be Jesus.[1]

One person who struggled with understanding Jesus was Peter. Jesus asks Peter, "Who do people say that I am?" Peter answers, giving a host of identities, a prophet or John the Baptist. Then Jesus says, "But Peter, who do you say that I am?" Peter says, "You are the Christ, the Son of the living God." Bingo! Peter gets the title of Jesus right. But then Jesus goes on to clarify what the Son of God must do: be rejected, suffer, die, and be buried. Peter does not like this interpretation and basically tells Jesus he's wrong. Jesus responds even more forcefully, saying to Peter, "Get behind me, Satan" (Mark 8:33). Peter could not get the identity of Jesus right. Peter knew that Jesus was the Christ. He just did not want the Christ to suffer and die. Peter resisted the identity of Jesus. Jesus was Jesus when he taught, cured the sick, drew huge crowds, and performed miracles. Jesus was going to be a success story, or so Peter thought. Peter could not anticipate the Last Supper, the agony in the garden, the trial, and the cross. Peter is going to spend the entire Gospel narrative learning what it means for Jesus to be the Christ. Not until the resurrection did Peter begin to fathom who Jesus is. And then the evangelist John on the beach describes Jesus confronting Peter and us with what exactly it means to get the story of Jesus right (John 21:1–25). Getting the story of Jesus right means giving up, as Peter finally did, on all the safe and protective assumptions that keep us from knowing Jesus as he is.

The stories of the scriptures can transform us so that we can get the identity of Jesus right. For that to happen, we need to let the scriptures speak to us so that we can understand who Jesus is. If we let Jesus be who he is, then the scriptures will not only give us ideas, but they will actually transform us.

One of the leading liberation theologians, Father Jon Sobrino, stayed with me several years ago. He lives in El Salvador. On November 16, 1989, in El Salvador, all the members of his community—six Jesuits and their housekeeper and her daughter—were brutally murdered. Jon was in Asia speaking when the assassinations occurred.

Jon lectured here at Boston College and his central message was that we remember the Jesus of history. Why? Because Jesus died on the cross. The one whom we call our Lord and Savior was completely abandoned and vilified. Before he became the Christ in glory, Jesus was the one hanging on a cross.

How could this happen? Why did it happen? These are questions that Sobrino asks us. These are some of the most important questions in Christian faith. How could the Lord of history end up abandoned and executed in an ignominious way?

Like others, Sobrino wants us to get the story of the historical Jesus right so that we can truly follow the Christ of faith. He wants us to get the story right so that we may know how to follow him—that is, to be disciples of Jesus.

If we get the story of Jesus right, and if we want to follow in his footsteps, what else do we need to do?

THE GIFTS OF FAITH, HOPE, AND CHARITY

For Christians, the life of Jesus does not end with the cross. We believe that Jesus is raised from the dead, not as in a resuscitation, but as in living eternally in glory. He is the first born of the new creation.

We believe that we too will be raised in glory, but we also believe that along the way of discipleship, Christ helps us. One fundamental way that we are assisted is by faith: the Christ of faith gives us faith. Faith is a gift. We do not believe because we simply decide to believe. Rather, we receive from Christ the invitation to believe, and from Christ we receive the grace, the divine ability, to believe.

In faith, then, we follow Jesus Christ. Yet even the call to follow Jesus and even the ability to be a disciple come from Christ. He calls us to follow him; he gives us the grace to follow him. In short, Christ makes it possible for us to follow him.

Certainly we need to give our assent to the call of Christ to follow him, but the call itself is first from God. God wills us to follow Christ. We are called. But then in order to be good disciples we need God's assistance and this is what grace is about—the divine gift to help us on the way to salvation.

Three gifts of grace are the virtues of faith, hope, and charity. By faith we are able to believe in God and in Jesus Christ. Faith is the foundation of the Christian life: by faith we believe in the Trinity, our creation, the incarnation, redemption, the true nature of Jesus Christ, the Kingdom of God, and eternal life.

It is important to understand that faith is not knowledge. Faith is our being able to believe, until we see God face to face, that God is, that God loves, and that God saves. Until we have knowledge, that knowledge that we only have in glory, then we only can believe by the grace that God gives us.

Like faith, hope is to have confidence for things not yet seen. Hope, too, is a gift. Sometimes people think of Christian hope as something easy, but that's not Christian hope. I think Christian hope is very difficult, for we hope when it is easier not to hope. Christian hope is our aid in the face of adversity. By hope, we believe we will attain what even now seems so unattainable. I think it is important to see that Christian hope begins at the cross of Jesus. Christian hope was born as Jesus breathed his last. We are not foolish in hope; rather, we are realists. We understand how terrible death is, but we still hope. We understand the challenges of life, but we believe that by hope we can meet and overcome those challenges. Our hope is not a way that we are naive about our expectations; rather Christian hope is found in the grief of a Christian who knows that a loved one has died but still, despite all the evidence, looks to be reunited with the loved one in glory.

Finally, there is charity, the experience of being in union with God, oneself, and one another. Jesus gave us a command to love, but charity makes it possible for us to follow that command. Charity is our union with God in Jesus Christ. By charity we understand and are able to love God, our neighbor, and ourselves. By charity we realize that like God, we are called simply to love, but love is not easy. The virtue of charity helps us to love when we would rather not.

These gifts from the Christ of faith are accompanied by the Holy Spirit. We remember from the scriptures that after the death and resurrection of Jesus, the Holy Spirit descended onto the disciples at Pentecost and gave them the ability to believe, to hope, and to love. The Holy Spirit accompanies us as we follow the Lord of history.

Together these virtues make us free to follow Christ and to do the will of God. We are made free by these gifts of grace. And here we return to the beginning of this chapter because it is important to realize that only after the death and resurrection of Jesus, and then the descent of the Holy Spirit, does Peter get the narrative right. No matter how hard Peter tried, it was only with the grace of Christ in glory and the assistance of the Holy Spirit that Peter would be able to understand what it meant for Jesus to be the Christ. Once Peter understood that, Peter was free to preach Jesus Christ and to follow him.

We get the identity of Jesus right when we too receive the three theological virtues, as they are called, and the presence of the Holy Spirit. When we receive these gifts we truly begin to follow him, for by these gifts we actually see him as he goes ahead of us. When we follow Jesus, we find ourselves on the way of Jesus.

THE BEATITUDES

I used to think that the three theological virtues were all we needed to follow Christ, but then my friend Lúcás Chan kept insisting that I needed to see the moral relevance of the Beatitudes. Of course, he was right. But what Lúcás helped me to understand was that these were not sayings that helped me to understand what I needed to do. He helped me to understand that these attributes in the Beatitudes were key features of the identity of Jesus. They make sense only if I see them as filling out the image of the one we wish to follow. In a way these are the attributes for those who want to enter the

Kingdom of God, for the Kingdom of God is no other than Jesus himself. These attributes for the disciple are the very identifying traits of the master.

Lúcás was not the only one making these claims. Augustine claimed that the Sermon on the Mount was the complete, perfect teaching of Christian morality. More recently, Pope John Paul II pointed out in his encyclical *Veritatis Splendor* that the Beatitudes belong to the Sermon on the Mount, which he called "the *magna charta* of Gospel morality."[2] There he added that the Beatitudes are "a sort of *self-portrait of Christ.*"[3]

Rightly, Lúcás chooses Matthew 5:3–12. Matthew's Gospel proposes the Beatitudes as a way of following Jesus Christ, who is preparing us for the Kingdom of God: he is giving us a blueprint, both personally and communally, of the attributes we need to enter the kingdom that Jesus is bringing in. Moreover the Beatitudes have a coherence, a coherence, however, that is dynamic in that for Lúcás, as for other scholars, the attributes build one upon another until finally one realizes that he is climbing a ladder of ascent. From the beginning they look perfectionistic, but once one begins to take the first few steps, one realizes that each step, in a way, empowers the other. It is like any notion of personal or communal growth: until we begin the program we really are not able to see where the program is taking us. This "ladder-like" approach was in fact named such by early Church Fathers, most notably John Climacus (579–649).

Here are the Eight Beatitudes in Matthew's Gospel:

1. Blessed are the poor in spirit, for theirs is the kingdom of heaven.
2. Blessed are they who mourn, for they shall be comforted.
3. Blessed are the meek, for they shall inherit the earth.
4. Blessed are they who hunger and thirst for righteousness, for they shall be satisfied.
5. Blessed are the merciful, for they shall obtain mercy.
6. Blessed are the pure of heart, for they shall see God.
7. Blessed are the peacemakers, for they shall be called children of God.
8. Blessed are they who are persecuted for the sake of righteousness, for theirs is the kingdom of heaven.

The First Beatitude, Matthew 5:3

Blessed are the poor in spirit, for theirs is the kingdom of heaven.

For the first beatitude, "the poor in spirit," Lúcás with other biblical theologians, or exegetes, insists that these poor are not only spiritually so; as one who grew up in poverty, he writes that the word Matthew uses for poor means "beggar." They are socially and economically needy and dependent. Their condition is such that being without everything, they are in special need of God's help. He adds, "the poor in spirit who often suffer from economic poverty are those who acquire the internal attitude of humility."[4]

Lúcás notes that the condition "poor in spirit" prompts one to develop an attitude of being "poor in spirit." The attitude is the equivalent of the virtue of humility. Lúcás points out that this humility is a spiritual emptying out; he writes, "humility means accepting the complete poverty of our human condition."[5] This is what the poor in spirit experience: only in God do they find their needs met. Discarded by all in society, reduced to begging, they have only God as their hope and to God they come suppliant.

Lúcás sees that this attitude of the poor in spirit can be emulated. For each of the beatitudes, Lúcás begins the section on ethics by first naming a virtue that expresses the particularity of the beatitude. He then offers how the virtue functions, what practices express it, who exemplifies it, and what is the social context that most needs the virtue.

For the first beatitude, Lúcás underlines how for many, from Church Fathers like Climacus, John Chrysostom, Ambrose, and Augustine to contemporary theologians like Gerald Vann and Johannes Metz, all found humility, to have an attitude of being poor in spirit, as the foundation of any Christian anthropology. The practices of humility begin with the acknowledgment of God as the ultimate source and meaning of our lives, which leads us to renounce anything that separates us from God. This requires an ability to be both detached as well as free to share what we have, and both depend on ascetical practices of self-denial. Exemplars begin with Jesus, who tells us, "Take my yoke upon you, and learn from me, for I am gentle and humble of heart" (Matt. 11:29).

Unfortunately, many think of humility as self-loathing or as self-deprecating. But humility is never false. Only the person that realizes their worth can be humble: like the beggar, who begs knowing their worth, expecting us to give. I think of true humility as knowing one's place in God's world, like Mary in the Magnificat (Luke 1:46–55). Mary sings out, "The Lord has done great things for me and Holy is God's Name." Humility then points to God, not to oneself. It is the opposite of narcissism. Narcissus looks in the water and falls in love with himself. The humble person looks in the mirror and sees God at work in himself.

The Second Beatitude, Matthew 5:4

Blessed are they who mourn, for they shall be comforted.

As in the chapters on the Ten Commandments, Lúcás begins each chapter of the Beatitudes with, "What did the text proclaim?" For the second beatitude, Lúcás notes how Matthew states that the promise for his mourners is that they will be comforted, while Luke's mourners will laugh. At the start, Lúcás wants to know what these blessed people are mourning? Again he turns to exegetes who suggest that grieving in the second beatitude is directed to the poor in the first.

Lúcás is aware of the banality of many ethicists and preachers who insist that the beatitude is a summons to mourn, but Lúcás notes, "no one is being told to mourn!"[6] They are already mourning. Ignoring this insight, these preachers insist on saying that Christ is counseling us to mourn, for if one denies one's own grief, one will never know the comfort and happiness that follows. In other words, the second beatitude is a cheap summons to grief counseling.

Reminding us of the ladder of ascent, Lúcás takes us to see that we are mourning not for our losses but for our brothers and sisters in the first beatitude who are beggars, abject in their poverty of spirit. Note that we are not mourning for those who elect a poverty of spirit, but rather for those whose condition is so bereft of any human good.

Lúcás writes, "The object of mourning is not so much one's own suffering or sins, but rather the concrete human experience of poverty and suffering encountered by community members. Mourning points to an other-oriented moral value."[7] Then emphatically he adds: "Such is the lot of the disciples of Christ—when our brothers and sisters suffer, we cannot help but mourn. This is very different from other interpretations of the beatitude, such as the 'call to console' proposed by Häring. The beatitude is not about that; it is about a certain disposition that genuine disciples have with one another, such that if one suffers, the other mourns as well."[8]

When Lúcás looks for an apt virtue, solidarity naturally appears as the virtue of the second beatitude. The practice related to solidarity is not comfort, but rather mourning itself. "In mourning the self tries to identify with the other. Mourning is then the ready subordination of one's own comfort and well being to the suffering of others." He adds, "In this way, one allows one's private life to be touched by the pain and suffering of the other."[9]

Lúcás is not calling us to a maudlin practice. Rather, grieving is an "other-center attitude," a way that one trains one's own capacity for solidarity with the other by entering into the experience of the other's lot and loss. Not until I fully grasp the loss of the other can I resonate with the condition of my sibling who is poor. So mourning is itself "a truthful expression of the virtue of solidarity."[10]

Listening is a very fine practice for those who mourn in solidarity with another. It allows one to grasp what the other's condition is. For one who suffers, it is so important to be able to find one's voice and to be able to speak one's own grief and loss. Listening allows the other to speak, to say the harsh things that no one wants to hear. Listening allows the sufferer to express the disappointment, the abandonment, the hurt, and the misery. When we hear their lament we inevitably mourn and enter more deeply into another's condition. So many who suffer are looking to be heard.

You may say, yes, but they want a reply! Of course they do. But you who are mourning are only learning the ascent of the Beatitudes. You have other steps to go before you can begin to do the work of protest in the fourth beatitude or the work of righteousness in the eighth beatitude. Christ is teaching us to ascend to a capacity to work for these on the first. Now being humble and in solidarity, we must move to the third beatitude.

The Third Beatitude, Matthew 5:5

Blessed are the meek, for they shall inherit the earth.

Climbing the ladder further, Lúcas takes us to the third beatitude, the meek who will inherit the earth. Here he surveys the work of biblical theologians, or exegetes as they are known, since their work of understanding the meaning of a text is called "exegesis." He uncovers how inclusive the term is. First, it appears often in the Septuagint (those texts from the Hebrew Bible that are put into a Greek edition) as a word for the *anawim*, the poor, the remnant, those completely left behind. In other words, the meek are again effectively the poor in spirit. Secondly, meekness is also an attribute of biblical leadership, first focusing on Jesus but also on others in the community (Matt. 11:29; Luke 7:36–50; 1 Pet. 3:4; Titus 3:2). Third, meekness is an ethical attribute of leadership elsewhere. In Jewish literature, meekness marks the sage and the ruler. In Greek literature, it marks the quality of both the true philanthropist and the true philosopher. Meekness is certainly an attribute for a fairly inclusive group of people.

As in the first beatitude, we see how an attitude emerges from a condition, but that this attitude that emerges from the poor can be appropriated by others. Lúcas writes, "While the term 'meek' as a condition tends to refer to the poor, the powerless, and those who mourn, as a moral attitude it considers also the rich and powerful."[11]

Meekness becomes for us a transformative virtue, especially as it tempers those whose anger tends toward violence or those whose power moves toward domination. Meekness finds its correlative in gentleness and therefore in this sense, Lúcas suggests that we see meekness tempering arrogance in the powerful; he writes, "The virtue of meekness helps transform our desire to dominate into a vital force to serve."[12] In this way we can see how we can "emphasize it as a virtue for the poor and the powerful." Here he turns to Monika Hellwig's astute observation that the powerful "need to unlearn those patterns of behavior that control and dominate others and that 'defend' their possessions and prestige at the cost of others."[13] In a fairly remarkable application to social context, Lúcas also explores how meekness would look alive in the corporate world.

When the powerful become champions of justice, they need to develop interiorly a new modesty, an ability to stand as one among others, as one not expecting the head place at the table. Meekness allows the powerful to enter the community as a member instead of as its leader. Meekness allows the powerful to use their power gently, not narcissistically, but compassionately—that is, truly in an other-directed way. Meekness tames the powerful so that their work is truly righteous. Without meekness, they are in no way able to inherit the earth.

We could follow through on the remaining five beatitudes, but what is so refreshing in each of these instances (most beatitudes are treated by Lúcás exegetically and ethically in five or six pages) are the ways Lúcás engages the double competency. In the fourth beatitude, for instance, knowing the biblical investigations he appreciates that "God's righteousness as revealed in Scripture is very different from our contemporary understanding of justice." To get us to a right understanding of what we are to strive for, Lúcás, who taught on three continents (Asia, Europe, and North America), tries to coax us from our assumptions and tries to lead us to understanding what exactly the text might mean and why that makes a difference for how we should live as Christians. Once we understand why we should strive for the righteousness of God, Lúcás leads us to understand fortitude as the virtue of the fourth beatitude.

CONCLUSION

In the United States, one of the greatest Christian ethicists is James Gustafson. He has influenced the field, directing doctoral candidates in Christian ethics at Yale, Chicago, and Emory Universities. Gustafson proposes two perspectives on how to best understand the New Testament by way of the categories, revealed morality and revealed reality.[14]

Reading the New Testament through the lens of revealed morality means that we are seeking to figure out if the text "reveals" a new code of ethics by which we should live. Certainly, the New Testament gives us the new law. it promulgates the love commandment (Matt. 22:34–40; Mark 12:28–34; Luke 10:25–28). But does it reveal many other ethical and moral codes? Jesus, for instance, says no divorce (Mark 10:11–12; Luke 16:18), but then Matthew's Gospel raises an exception (Matt. 5:31–32), and later Paul raises his own as well (1 Cor. 7:12–16). Is this revealed morality?

What about dietary laws? After all, the Old Testament had over six hundred laws and many of them were dietary. Are these revealed laws, laws of revealed morality? Or what about sex before marriage? Is there any revealed morality about this issue in the New Testament? Or even on abortion? A long line of questions arises, including: Should women be treated equal to men? How should children be treated? Again and again the question arises: Where are the New Testament laws about the issues we face every day?

As we ask more and more questions about contemporary issues, like stem-cell research, cloning, gender equity, class differentiation, democratic values, and so on, we find fewer and fewer instances of the scriptures instructing us with laws of revealed morality.

With all these questions and so few clear answers, many moral theologians look at the other alternative as providing a better context for understanding how God's will is conveyed. They talk about a revealed reality in which our lives and our world are illuminated by the Gospels. Here we are invited to look at reality in a new way: the mercy of God redeeming the world through the life, death, and resurrection of Jesus. Then, in the light of God's revelation, we formulate our code of ethics through our reason, experience, and the tradition that binds us to those before and after us.

So which alternative do you prefer? Revealed morality with laws straight from God? Or revealed reality that provides a context for articulating the laws that we believe God wants us to live by?

Fortunately, by being Roman Catholics we do not have to choose because Catholics invariably avoid "either/or" options and pursue instead "both/and" approaches. As we saw in the beginning of this chapter, our understanding of the Jesus of history helps inform our understanding of the Christ of faith, and vice versa. We recognize clearly that our world is illuminated by the Gospels and that we live in a time that is already the reign of God, though not yet. Our reality is being transformed as is our self-understanding. But we also see that, as a matter of fact, God's will is clearly expressed in a variety of utterances: for instance, the love commandment and the works of mercy in the Last Judgment (Matt. 25:31–46). In short, we see that specific teachings illuminate our world and this illumination helps us to discover what it is in our daily life that God calls from us.

STUDY QUESTIONS

1. What is your (main) image of God? Why do you think it is so important for you?
2. Do you believe that Jesus died for you? What does this mean?
3. Jesus calls you to be his disciple. What does discipleship mean to you?
4. There have been numerous movies about Jesus: *The Passion of the Christ, Jesus of Nazareth, King of Kings, The Greatest Story Ever Told, Jesus of Montreal*, and so on. Which movie have you found to be a good way of treating the life, death, and resurrection of Jesus?
5. What do you think of the distinction between the Jesus of history and the Christ of faith?
6. What do the Beatitudes mean to you? Where do you see yourself on their ladder of ascent?

Chapter Seven

Practicing the Corporal Works of Mercy

Is there something about Catholic morality that distinguishes it from the morality of other religious believers? This is a vexing question. This is not a question about superiority. It is simply a question about distinctiveness or uniqueness. In a word, it is the question about *identity*, about what identifies us as Catholics in our moral living.

The question is vexing because it is difficult to find one thing that belongs to Catholics as Catholics. For instance, we Catholics appreciate the natural law. But in Romans 1, St. Paul says that the natural law is written in everyone's heart; by that law, people can tell right from wrong. Because of this, many Catholics believe that what is right for Catholics is right for everyone and whatever is wrong for Catholics is equally wrong for everyone.

Others root our morality in the scriptures. Here we think, of course, of the Ten Commandments. But these are shared with Jews, Protestants, and Orthodox Christians. Moreover, these commandments are pretty comprehensive. From them we receive moral guidance regarding the sovereignty of God and God's name; worship; honoring parents; cherishing life, our bodies, and the truth; respecting neighbors, their families, and their property. The commandments cover most moral topics.

Despite the fact that the natural law provides all human beings access to the same moral standards and that the Ten Commandments offer those of us in the Judeo-Christian tradition a fundamental morality that has affected the foundations of morality throughout the Western world, still I want to say unequivocally that we Catholics have defined ourselves distinctively in our moral lives and that distinctiveness is found in the virtue of mercy. While in the most recent generations we may not have formed ourselves as explicitly according to mercy (which I define as the willingness to enter into the chaos of others so as to answer them in their need), still, as we shall see, the life of the Catholic Church has been to form us according to mercy.

While fellow Protestants recognize the extraordinary importance of mercy as the basic stance of our God toward us, we Catholics have taken that insight further in terms of a long legacy of the corporal works of mercy—feed the hungry, give drink to the thirsty, shelter the homeless, clothe the naked, visit the sick, visit the imprisoned, and bury the dead—and the spiritual works of mercy—give good counsel, teach the ignorant, admonish sinners, console the afflicted, pardon offenses and injuries, bear offenses patiently, and pray for the living and the dead. Those works have distinguished us, for if there is one dimension of the Christian tradition that differentiates Protestants from Catholics, it is precisely "works."

MERCY IN THE CATHOLIC TRADITION

To make my case for the central distinctiveness of mercy, I want to give four instances that highlight the centrality of mercy.

First, the Good Samaritan parable portrays neighbor love definitively as the practice of mercy. We remember why Jesus tells this parable. He has just given the commandment to love one another. In response, one of the scribes asks Jesus, "Who is my neighbor?" Jesus responds by telling the parable of the Good Samaritan (Luke 10:25–37). The parable tells the story of a man robbed and left wounded outside the city gates on the road to Jericho. A priest and a scribe each pass him by, rushing to get to their respective appointments. The only one to stop to attend to the man is a Samaritan, a person considered foreign to the Jewish people. The Samaritan treats the man's wounds, takes him to a nearby inn, pays in part for his stay at the inn, and promises to pay the full bill and to take the man with him when he returns.

A close reading of the story reveals that Jesus is offering a very surprising answer to the question. At the beginning of the story we are thinking that the answer to the question "Who is my neighbor?" is the man lying wounded on the road. But by the end of the story we are no longer looking at the neighbor who is wounded but rather at the neighbor who is acting. The scribe therefore answers that the neighbor is the one who shows mercy. In the beginning we think the parable is about whom we should assist. But the end is really about who we are called to be. We are called to be like the Good Samaritan—that is, to be a neighbor.

Like the surprising ending, many of us forget that this parable was never primarily a moral one. Starting with Clement of Alexandria (ca. 150–ca. 215), then Origen (ca. 184–ca. 254), Ambrose (339–390), and finally Augustine (354–430), the Good Samaritan parable is the merciful narrative of our redemption. Later from Venerable Bede (673–735) to Martin Luther

(1483–1546), preachers and theologians appropriate and modify the narrative, but in each instance, the narrative is first and foremost not about us, but rather about Jesus! They wrote that the wounded man who lies outside the gates is Adam, wounded by sin, fallen, outside the gates of Eden. The priest and the Levite, representing the tradition and the law, are unable to do anything for Adam. Along comes the Good Samaritan, the Christ, a foreigner, one not from here, who tends to Adam's wounds, takes him to the inn (which is the church), gives a down payment (which is his life) for Adam's healing or salvation, and promises to return for him (the second coming), when he will pay in full for the redemption and take him with him into his kingdom.

The parable then is first and foremost not a story about how we should treat others, but rather the story of what Christ has done for us. We are called to follow the actions of the Good Samaritan not because the parable is an attractive one, but because it is a retelling of the entire Gospel.

The parable is not, then, one among many; it serves as the foundational explanation of the love commandment. As William Spohn notes, it has a privileged position in the Gospels and a privileged position in the church that hears the Gospel proclaimed.[1]

This leads to the second point—namely, that the scriptures name mercy as the condition for salvation. This is made clear in the Last Judgment in Matthew 25, where those are saved because they performed what we later called the corporal works of mercy, which we named above.

The parable of Matthew 25 is striking in that everyone is surprised by the judgment. Let us remember the parable. The King is there and the goats and sheep stand before him. The goats are condemned to hell. "Why?" ask the goats. The King responds, "Because you did not feed me when I was hungry, clothe me when I was naked," and so forth. The goats say, "But when did we see you hungry, or naked?" The King says, "What you did not do for the least, you did not do to me." Similarly the King summons the sheep to enter his Kingdom. "Why?" ask the sheep. The King says, "Because you fed me when I was hungry, clothed me when I was naked," and so forth. "When did we do that?" they ask. And the King answers, "Whenever you did it for the least, you did it to me." Thus, while the sheep never realized that in feeding the hungry they were feeding the King, unfortunately the goats never realized that by not visiting the sick, they were not visiting the Lord.

For the Gospel writers, we will be judged by whether we practiced mercy, and we will not be excused if we knew not to practice it. Often the Gospels remind us that we should know that we should be merciful. We saw, for instance, how Jesus contrasted the Good Samaritan with the priest and the scribe who pass by the wounded man. In Luke 16:19–31, Jesus tells the parable of the rich man who steps over and ignores the daily pleas of poor Lazarus, begging at the rich man's gates. When the rich man dies and is sent to Hades, he asks for relief, but the Lord says, "You ignored Lazarus for his whole life." Like the goats, the rich man in Luke 6 learns this "moral" in Hades: he never showed mercy to poor Lazarus begging at his gate. The practice of mercy, whether we know it or not, is the measure of our judgment.

Third, our entire theological tradition is expressed in terms of mercy—that is, the willingness to enter into the chaos of others so as to answer them in their need. Like the Good Samaritan stopping for wounded Adam, attending to someone in need is no simple affair. Helping anyone in need is entering into the entire "problem" or "chaos" of their situation.

Thus, the creation is bringing order out of the chaos of the universe, the incarnation is God's entry into the chaos of human existence, and the redemption is bringing us out of the chaos of our slavery to sin. Christ's own entrance into the chaos of death occasions our hope in the risen life, and his pledge to return again is a pledge to deliver us from the chaos of our own lives. Every action of God is aimed at rescuing us. One of my favorite understandings of God's rescue of us comes from the meditation on the Trinity in the *Spiritual Exercises* of St. Ignatius. In it, the three persons of the blessed Trinity consider the chaos of the world wherein most people are going to hell. They decide that we must be saved: one of the persons will enter into our lives to keep us from all falling into the abyss of hell, itself pure chaos.

Fourth, early Christianity defined itself by the practice of mercy. In *The Rise of Christianity*, Rodney Stark argues that "Christianity was an urban movement, and the New Testament was set down by urbanites."[2] Those urban areas were dreadful. Stark describes the conditions in those areas as "social chaos and chronic urban misery." This chaos resulted in part from population density. At the end of the first century, Antioch's population was 150,000 within the city walls, or 117 persons per acre. By way of comparison, New York City has a density of thirty-seven persons per acre, and Manhattan with its high-rise apartments has one hundred persons per acre. Moreover, contrary to common assumptions, Greco-Roman cities were not settled places whose inhabitants descended from previous generations. With high infant mortality and relatively brief life expectancy, these cities required "a constant and substantial stream of newcomers" in order to maintain their population levels. As a result, the cities were largely composed of strangers. These strangers were well treated by early Christians, many of whom, again contrary to assumptions, were anything but poor. Through a variety of ways of caring for newcomers, financially secure Christians welcomed the newly arrived immigrants.

Moreover, their religion was new. Certain demands were imposed by the gods of the pagan religions. But these demands were substantively ritual; they were not neighbor directed. And while pagan Romans knew generosity, that generosity did not stem from any divine command. A nurse who cared for a victim of an epidemic knew that her life might be lost. If she were a pagan, there was no expectation of divine reward for her generosity; if she were a Christian, however, she believed that she would be rewarded in the next life for having done what God commanded in this life.

The religion was new to the Roman Empire, therefore, because the Christian God required mercy to be practiced toward all who called upon the name of the Lord. Christianity required the recognition of the stranger in need as neighbor and, inevitably, as sibling; Christianity commanded the Christian to embrace faithfully the one in need of mercy. Stark writes:

> This was the moral climate in which Christianity taught that mercy is one of the primary virtues—that a merciful God requires humans to be merciful. Moreover, the corollary (that *because* God loves humanity, Christians may not please God unless they *love one another*) was entirely new. Perhaps even more revolutionary was the principle that Christian love and charity must extend beyond the boundaries of family and tribe, that it must extend to "all those who in every place call on the name of our Lord Jesus Christ" (1 Cor. 1:2). . . . This was revolutionary stuff. Indeed, it was the cultural basis for the revitalization of a Roman world groaning under a host of miseries.[3]

These four reasons (the paradigm for neighbor love in the Good Samaritan parable, the Gospels' demand for mercy as the condition for our salvation, the writing of our entire theological tradition in the key of mercy, and the actual historical rootedness of our church in the merciful practices of first-century Christians) place mercy in a privileged position for identifying the Roman Catholics as such.

The centrality of the practice of mercy in the moral life of the church cannot be overlooked. It ranks among the activities that best describe the moral life of the church: the confession of sins, obeying the Ten Commandments, developing the virtues, and practicing the corporal and spiritual works of mercy.

Mercy is so important because it is, above all, the experience we have of God. In response to that mercy, we become imitators of the God in whose image we are made. Likewise, in answer to Christ's call to follow him, we practice mercy. Thomas Aquinas asks the question whether mercy is the greatest virtue (*Summa Theologiae* II.II.30.4) and responds that charity is the greatest virtue because by it we are united in love to God, but, second to charity, mercy is the greatest because by it we exemplify God in God's actions and, therefore, we become like God.

THE EARLY TRADITION OF THE CORPORAL WORKS OF MERCY

Much could be written about how the corporal works of mercy developed as such. As noted above, today we know the seven that are part of our tradition: feed the hungry, give drink to the thirsty, shelter the homeless, clothe the naked, visit the sick, visit the imprisoned, and bury the dead. These are later paired with the spiritual works: give good counsel, teach the ignorant, admonish sinners, console the afflicted, pardon offenses and injuries, bear offenses patiently, and pray for the living and the dead.

While the first six of the corporal works of mercy are found in the Last Judgment parable in Matthew 25:34–45, it took several centuries for the final articulation of these seven to become a cornerstone of the Christian life. Eventually they paralleled other groups of seven like the sacraments, the deadly sins, and the virtues (the four cardinal—fortitude, temperance, justice, and prudence—and three theological—faith, hope, and love).

Before the set mantra of seven was firmly situated, Christians heard the divine injunction to practice mercy. John never tires of recommending it (e.g., 1 John 4:20–21). Luke tells us how deacons are appointed to serve the most marginalized (Acts 6:1–6). Paul writes to Timothy about the selection of widows who, like the deacons, are to serve those in need (1 Tim. 5:9–10). Collectively and institutionally, the apostolic church promoted the service of mercy.

Almsgiving became an early expression of mercy. In the apostolic age, the practice of the collection began when Paul instructed the Corinthians to set aside a collection for the first day of every week (1 Cor. 16:1–2), presumably during the Eucharist. Later Clement writes: "Almsgiving is good as a penance for sin; fasting is better than prayer, but almsgiving is better than both, and charity covers a multitude of sins" (2 Clem. 16).

These many calls to mercy were heeded. For instance, Cyprian, bishop of Carthage, led his congregation to respond to victims of the plague in 252. Bishop Dionysius provided a narrative of his community's response to the plague in Alexandria in 259: "Most of our brethren, in their surpassing charity and brotherly love did not spare themselves and clinging to one another fearlessly visited the sick and ministered to them. Many, after having nursed and consoled the sick, contracted the illness and cheerfully departed this life. The best of our brethren died in this way, some priests and deacons, and some of the laity" (Eusebius, *History of the Church*, 7.22.9).

Why is the call to mercy made? Normally, six motives are found in the writings of the scriptures and among the fathers. First, Proverbs 15:27 encourages us to practice mercy for the remission of our sins—that is, in gratitude for God's merciful stance toward our sinfulness. John Chrysostom (344?–407) sees mercy here as the queen of the virtues outweighing all our burdensome sins.[4]

Second, Tobit 12:8–9 tells us that for our prayers to be heard by God, works of mercy should accompany them. Several of the fathers (Augustine [354–430], Cyprian [d. 258], Leo the Great [d. 461], and John Chrysostom) preached on this theme.

Third, Matthew 6:20 suggests that works of mercy will lead to eternal reward, a motivation that Augustine often used.

Fourth, Matthew 25:40 reveals to us that any merciful action is for the sake of the Lord. Cyprian called this the most powerful of all motives, and here many of the fathers promoted the figures of Mary of Bethany and Zacchaeus as models of mercy. Similarly, the celebrated episode of Martin of Tours (316?–397) giving his cloak to the beggar became a motif throughout the church.

Fifth, Lactantius (ca. 250–ca. 325) and Ambrose (340?–397) urge mercy to fortify human solidarity and to extend the circle of fellowship in the Lord. Finally, Clement of Alexandria (d. 215), John Chrysostom, and Leo the Great remind us that works of mercy bring us into the life of perfection; by practicing mercy we become more like the God who entered into our own chaos.

In short, the claim of mercy engages some of the most fundamental interests that Catholics have.

THE PRACTICE OF MERCY IN THE MIDDLE AGES AND THE RENAISSANCE

In the Middle Ages, the monasteries became centers of the practice of mercy. One account from the famed monastery at Cluny, for instance, informs us that seventeen thousand persons were cared for in one year. Among the Cistercians, every abbey had a guest house for pilgrims, travelers, and the poor. There the abbot waited on them after welcoming them first by prostrating himself at their feet, for in welcoming the guest, the abbot welcomed Christ.

Besides the monks, many pious laypersons participated in the works of mercy by forming associations. These began in Naples in the tenth century and later appeared in Tuscany. By the twelfth century they were throughout France, Spain, and Italy, assisting the religious and mostly establishing and maintaining hospitals. For instance, in 1217 a hospital that once belonged to a religious community was handed over to a corporation of four priests, thirty laymen, and twenty-five laywomen. By the thirteenth and fourteenth centuries these activities were flourishing throughout Europe.

With the spirit of Francis and Dominic in the thirteenth century, many professional laypersons became inspired and answered with great imagination. For instance, in 1244 the head porter of a wool guild in Florence (Pier

Luca Borsi) formed the Company of Mercy with money collected by taxing colleagues for swearing. Others reached out to those suffering from leprosy. The Knights of St. Lazarus established three thousand hospitals for those suffering from the dreaded disease. Later, hospitals for the blind and for orphans were also founded.

One effect of the Crusades was the widespread practice of prostitution. In their aftermath, foundations were established to provide these women sanctuary; in turn, the women formed religious congregations. In the thirteenth century, for instance, the Congregation of the Penitents of St. Mary Magdalene had thirty communities throughout Europe.

By the sixteenth century, the establishment of guilds, along with the innovations of new religious orders like the Jesuits and the important reforms of the Council of Trent, provided new impetus for laypersons to belong to confraternities. These confraternities wed spiritual devotion with the practice of mercy. They had an enormous influence on the moral formation of Roman Catholics. Here let me mention only two. The Company of Divine Love was established to respond to those with syphilis, which broke out throughout Europe in the mid-1490s. Sufferers from this incurable disease were abandoned by families because of shame and by hospitals for fear of contagion. In 1499, the first hospital for the incurables was built in Genoa, then another in Rome, and others in Naples, Venice, and finally throughout Europe. The one in Rome, at the chapel of St. James on the Via Flaminia, served the needs of the pilgrims. That chapel and its *Hospedale degl' Incurabili* (Hospital for the Incurables) served the needs of those suffering from syphilis. The hospital became one of the most famous of Europe, where a variety of saints, from Camillus to Carlo Borromeo, served.

In 1498 Queen Eleanor of Portugal established the Confraternity of Misericordia. In 1516 it had one hundred members: fifty from the nobility, fifty from the working class, all dedicated to the fourteen works of mercy. By the queen's death in 1525 there were sixty-one branches of the confraternity. From the seventeenth to the nineteenth century, twenty-five confraternities were established in Portuguese colonies. Many still stand today.

ONE WORK: VISITING THE PRISONER

To appreciate the Catholic imagination at work in so many ways through the works of mercy, let us consider just one work: visiting the prisoner. This work has been practiced throughout the life of the church. Inasmuch as they were persecuted, church members visited their imprisoned brothers and sisters and worked to liberate them. Like Tertullian, Cyprian, and others, St. Ignatius of Antioch wrote (in his letter to the Christians of Smyrna), "When the Christians become aware that one of their number is a prisoner and suffering for the name of Christ, they take upon themselves all his needs and, if possible, they free him."

Early Christians routinely sought to comfort their fellow Christians who were imprisoned and sought their blessing as well. No less than Christ had been a prisoner. Thus, like Peter, Paul, and many of the apostles, imprisoned Christians were perceived as not only people in need but also people of courage and holiness. Working to visit, console, and liberate them were in themselves their own reward.

Clement of Rome tells us in his first chapter to the Corinthians that many ransomed others by offering themselves in exchange for the one held hostage.

Later in the twelfth century, a time of enormous spiritual and ecclesial developments, charitable institutions were established for the release of prisoners. The Trinitarians, founded by St. John of Malta, were singularly dedicated to ransoming prisoners and laboring to alleviate the conditions of those who remained in slavery. Similarly, the Order of Mercy was founded by St. Peter Nolasco for the same task.

In another period of spiritual renewal, the sixteenth century, religious orders were founded and their members worked along with other ministries for the care and release of prisoners. The Jesuits, for instance, provided a variety of services. The Jesuit historian John O'Malley reminds us first that these prisoners were either debtors or those awaiting trial, sentencing, or execution. In Rome, for example, over half the imprisoned were debtors from the poorer classes; the others, awaiting trial, had not yet had their guilt established. Jesuits took care of the imprisoned by preaching, catechizing, and confessing the imprisoned, and bringing them food and alms. In Italy and Spain, Jesuits spent a great deal of time raising funds through begging so as to pay off the prisoners' creditors. Elsewhere they begged for money to ransom back prisoners taken by the Turks. Likewise, they preached against slave-taking raids.

Sometimes the Jesuits worked to improve the plight of prisons. In Palermo, for instance, a confraternity was founded based on one Jesuit's work to improve the sanitary conditions of prisoners. Another confraternity organized by the Jesuits, the Confraternity of the Imprisoned, was founded for laypersons in Rome, and it generated other confraternities in six other cities throughout Italy.[5]

Other confraternities of the laity also dedicated themselves to those in prison. In Rome, the Archconfraternity of Charity was specifically for those in captivity, as was the Confraternity of Pietà and Our Lady of Loretto in Milan. In France, confraternities such as the Work of Prisons in Marseilles and the Confraternity of Mercy in Lyons were solely dedicated to prisoners' needs, while the White Penitents and the Sisters of the Dominican Third Order were singularly dedicated to the needs of women prisoners.

Another confraternity, in Florence, was dedicated to prisoners awaiting execution, most of whom were political prisoners. They would visit the prisoners and spend the night with them before the execution, praying with them and helping them to identify with Jesus as a condemned prisoner. The following day, a confraternity member would walk to the gallows with each prisoner, walking ahead of him and holding a painted panel of the suffering Christ in front of his face so that the condemned man could keep his gaze fixed on Jesus instead of on the crowds or the executioners. Six hundred years later, Sister Helen Prejean provides the same support in her accompaniment of those who are sentenced to death for capital crimes: she attends their executions, telling them to look on her face and see the face of Christ. She details her work in her beautiful book, *Dead Man Walking.*[6]

From these experiences of the prisons, there grew subsequently numerous critical voices that protested the conditions and started movements of reform to correct conditions among the imprisoned in Spain, Italy, France, and England.

We cannot underestimate the relevance of these confraternities: hundreds of them took care of prisoners and captives; others were established for the care of the mentally ill as well as those who are unable to hear and/or speak. These confraternities are only paralleled by the extraordinary number of religious orders that themselves adopt a work of mercy to identify with its own charism.

I too am involved in prison ministry. Sister Maureen Clark, C.S.J., has been working in prison ministry for many years and currently visits, supports, listens to, and works with the women at the women's correctional facility in Framingham, Massachusetts. Several years ago, Maureen was looking for new clergy to preside at Sunday mass and one of her volunteer musicians, at that time a doctoral student of mine, promptly volunteered me.

My schedule is busy. But I decided that I wanted to go. Having grown up as the son of a New York City police detective, prisons have always been frightening places for me. They became more terrifying when my dad, who later was involved in the investigation of the Attica uprising, took me through that prison. As I walked through the cavernous, gray hallways, I became afraid that, by some accident, I would be left "inside."

Years later, while visiting a Jesuit friend in Southern California, he informed me that we were going to Tijuana to say mass in the city jail. He told me that this was the happiest task of his priestly ministry. He described the place as very confining and very chaotic and did not hesitate to let me know about the broad diversity of crimes for which these men were detained, from petty debts to kidnapping and murder. I remember entering the cell with all the fear of a young child, watching my friend greet, embrace, and chat with the mingling prisoners, while I rigidly stood by the makeshift altar, occasionally glancing (almost frantically) at the guards on the other side of the common area. The strongest memory I have of that place is that when the liturgy was over, the guards announced that they could not open the gates to let us out for another twenty to thirty minutes. My friend smiled, shrugged his shoulders, and went back to the prisoners. I stayed by the doors and waited. I was convinced I had been left "inside."

The invitation from Sister Maureen to come to Framingham was not, then, what I would have put on my annual wish list. Yet, in light of the many fears that I have had to face, I thought, why not this one? The situation would be different, after all. I would be in Framingham, not Tijuana or Attica.

I arrived and met Sister Maureen and about twenty volunteers who were among a group of about one hundred who take turns coming to the Sunday evening mass. They led me through the procedures. I had to leave my wallet, wristwatch, car keys, and cash in the lockers. I had to sign in. I had to wait (nearly an hour). I was searched. I was eventually allowed to pass through innumerable gates and doors to go to the room where the mass would be held.

The mass was extraordinarily consoling. The women were welcoming. About a hundred showed up. They set up the altar, checked the readings, joined the choir, or just sat and prayed. They wanted to pray, especially for their children and, yes, grandchildren as well as for their sister inmates. Their prayers were many. They enjoyed the liturgy.

But they were in prison and whatever personal freedom I had gained by facing my fear, I realized that their freedom was incredibly restricted. I especially understood this when one prayed for another younger woman who had a hearing the next day. The hearing was to determine whether she would be released earlier. There was an evident but quiet desperation on the faces of many as the prayer was uttered.

"Do you like this work?" I later asked Maureen. "I love these women," she answered.

PRACTICING MERCY TODAY

Today many persons speak of an emerging lay ministry. But during a variety of periods in the church's life, laypersons—animated both by their own God-given talents and by the fundamental experience of God's mercy—were ministers. Their legacy of leadership and service needs to be studied, for it was phenomenal. A proper place to find it is in the variety of associations and confraternities in both the medieval and Renaissance periods. In those times of spiritual richness and economic prosperity, times like our own, the laity, alongside clergy and religious, imitated the merciful ways of the Good Samaritan.

·

But we can think of more recent examples. Here the Society of St. Vincent de Paul easily comes to mind. Composed originally of six students in Paris in 1833, the group's founder, A. Frederic Ozanam (1813–1853), recognized the call to relieve need but also to address the cause of the need. For this reason he identified two virtues for the society: the call of charity and of justice. Today, many recognize in his writings on social justice an anticipation of the social encyclical *Rerum Novarum*.

Ozanam's society eventually expanded throughout the world. For instance, in 1845, a group of lay Catholics met in St. Louis and formed the first council in the United States. The society has grown to the point where it now numbers some six hundred thousand members worldwide and has a presence in 132 countries.

In other instances, the laity and the religious often collaborate on a variety of corporal works of mercy, and these works are much more institutional, with central administrations designed to service effectively the needs of those in chaos. If we look at health care in the United States today, we see about 13 percent of all hospital beds belonging to Catholic health care institutions. The Catholic Church is, therefore, the largest singular health care provider in the United States.

These health care centers were almost all founded by religious women. Their distinctive spiritualities grew into a legacy of care, adaptation, responsiveness, and inventiveness that continues to be active today. Still, with shifts in understanding the nature of religious life, many Catholics are opting to serve the church not in religious life but as laypersons. With diminishing numbers in their ranks, these religious orders are looking at a variety of ways of guaranteeing the future of their apostolic institutions while promoting their original charism. In a way, they are handing on to another population the ministry that they so ably led. Better, they are incorporating into their own original vision a partnership with others.

One example of such innovation is Catholic Health Initiatives (CHI). Their mission "is to nurture the healing ministry of the Church by bringing it new life, energy, and viability in the twenty-first century. Fidelity to the Gospel urges us to emphasize human dignity and social justice as we move toward the creation of healthier communities." A national not-for-profit health care organization, it is composed of sixty-three hospitals and forty-three long-term care, assisted-living, independent-living, and residential facilities. Its ministry is found in nineteen states. They serve sixty-four rural and urban communities and represent more than sixty-seven thousand employees.

Multiple congregations entered into a partnership that, in turn, engaged lay leaders as well and formed a system that models the future of ministry: a truly equal religious-lay partnership. Because of their commitment to promoting new models of health care ministry, the hallmark of CHI is their mission and ministry fund. This assists projects described as "collaborative," "innovative," and "transferable" that aim to address the root causes of illness in any of the communities they serve. Generating new offspring, CHI seeks to continue in a ministry that has always been known for its inventiveness and its responsiveness.

Whatever corporal work of mercy we think of, invariably we find its contemporary expression. If we were to think of sheltering the homeless, we can think of the sixty million refugees and displaced persons around the world. Within that enormous population, 80 percent are women and children. Catholic Relief Services, together with Caritas Internationalis, dedicate themselves to the diverse needs of these people. If we think of teenage runaways, Covenant House alone served over fifty thousand youth last year.

Many of these organizations are, like the hospitals and social services, simply Roman Catholic in identity. Others are predominantly Christian, like Bread for the World, or without any religious affiliation, like Amnesty International. But in each instance, these associations have a core mission; they often provide direct service, but also political advocacy in an attempt to get the social welfare states to respond to the citizens' needs. But the wisdom that their forerunners provide—in whatever work it was—continues to shape the practical agendas that these agencies pursue today.

People from all walks of life seek to enter into the chaos of another in a variety of ways. Despite this, the long legacy of religious orders, diocesan programs, lay associations, and confraternities has deeply embedded in the Roman Catholic tradition its distinctive trademark that promotes mercy above all practical virtues.

MERCY OR JUSTICE

Sometimes people get concerned that mercy means helping a person out, but justice means working for the structural changes that so often oppress people. Mercy, people fear, is temporary action and doesn't move for social change. But this chapter shows us otherwise. By getting involved in mercy, people understand why others are in chaos.

Mercy calls us to meet human beings in need. By meeting them, often we realize that their situation is compromised. We go to a prison—we realize the need for prison reform; we visit the homeless—we need to develop shelters. We go to the shelters, and we realize the shelters need to be changed, and so on.

In the real merciful engagement, we realize that by entering into the chaos of others we eventually have to face what causes that chaos. But usually we cannot know about those needs until we have a merciful engagement first.

I think people who work for justice without knowing and meeting those who are suffering often have presumptions for action that are not helpful. I think that acting from mercy allows us to meet people in need and in turn we are moved to justice. But beginning with justice, without first having a merciful encounter, strikes me as very uninformed.

I have watched students here at Boston College enter many different immersion programs. In most instances, in that merciful meeting with people who are suffering, students return convinced that they need somehow to choose a professional field that will serve the cause of advocacy and justice. Mercy leads them to justice. By encountering the other, they are able to be awakened to the call of justice.[7]

STUDY QUESTIONS

1. Do you think there are other more important issues that define us as Catholic, other than mercy?
2. I define mercy as the willingness to enter into the chaos of another. Do you agree with that?
3. How do you act mercifully without being condescending?
4. What works of mercy do you think are more appropriate for today's contemporary world?

Chapter Eight

Cultivating the Cardinal Virtues

In order to think about virtue, let us consider one of the chief proponents of the cardinal virtues—Thomas Aquinas. This great Renaissance theologian is an important resource from the tradition, and to appreciate him, we must consider not only his work, but his life and his context.

Yet, to appreciate the exceptional importance of the medieval Scholastics in general and the thirteenth-century *Summa Theologiae* of Thomas Aquinas in particular, we have to turn first to the work of twelfth-century ascetical theology that made possible Thomas's great work.

THE IMPORTANCE OF TWELFTH-CENTURY ASCETICAL THEOLOGY

We saw in the introductory chapter that, with few exceptions, the subject of moral theology was basically for assisting monks and priests to be good confessors. The penitentials, the confessional manuals, and the later moral manuals with their singular focus on sin were specifically distinguished from works of ascetical, spiritual, or devotional theology, which were about the pursuit of "perfection" or growing in the life of discipleship. If we recall the first principle of the natural law—that is, to avoid evil and to pursue the good—then moral theology was singularly concerned with the avoidance of evil and ascetical theology was about pursuing the good.

When we think of the history of ascetical theology,[1] we must inevitably turn to the twelfth century. "The twelfth century has long been seen as a turning point in the history of Latin spirituality," claims the great historian of Western spirituality, Bernard McGinn. "[T]here can be no argument that the twelfth century was fascinated with the mystery of the human person as *imago Dei*." Through the spiritual friendship of Aelred of Rievaulx

(1109–1167), the insistence on conscience by Abelard (1079–1142), the location of the image of God in human freedom by Bernard of Clairvaux (1090–1153), the knowledge of the way of the Lord and the appreciation of the goodness of the human body and the delight of the passions by Hildegard of Bingen (1098–1179), and the understanding of the interpersonal human subject as in the image of the three-personed God by Richard of St. Victor (1123–1173), the theologians of the twelfth century developed a powerful, relational understanding of the human as a foundation for their spirituality. [2]

Another great historian, Caroline Walker Bynum, agrees with McGinn: "No period was ever busier creating structures for its piety than the twelfth century." [3] Like McGinn, Bynum studies Bernard of Clairvaux, who with "other 'new monks' stressed discovery of self—and of self-love—as the first step in a long process of returning to the love and likeness of God, a love and likeness in which the individual is not dissolved into God but rather becomes God's partner and friend." [4] Bernard's spirituality as well as his contemporaries' drew deeply from the scriptures and cultivated in a particular way a devotion to the humanity of Jesus, which moved readers into greater intimacy with Jesus and with those who shared the devotion. [5] In developing a highly relational vision of the human, the twelfth century never compromised the person and in fact discovered "the self, the inner mystery, the inner man, the inner landscape." [6]

The discovery of the self did not mean, however, an endorsement of individualism; as Bynum argues, the twelfth century "also discovered the group in two very precise senses: it discovered that many separate 'callings' or 'lives' were possible in the church, and it elaborated a language for talking about how individuals became a part of them (the language of 'conforming to a model')." [7]

These various twelfth-century charismatic persons, who discovered not only the "person" but also the "group," were the forerunners of the great religious orders founded in the thirteenth century. In fact, in many ways, their appreciation of humanity as being in the image of the Trinity—that is, as being in the image of the triune God—becomes the foundation of the entire Renaissance.

I first tasted the Renaissance in 1981 by studying Italian in Florence so as to prepare for doctoral studies in Rome. I went there with a wonderful guide, my friend the historian John O'Malley. I remember when we first entered that incredible art collection in the Uffizi Gallery. There, in the very first room, I saw the birth of the Renaissance: three enormous canvases of the Madonna enthroned surrounded by angels presenting the Godhead in the human person of her infant son, Jesus. Here was the glory of God in the human fully alive and here were Duccio, Cimabue, and Giotto presenting their masterpieces. In the birth of Jesus, the Renaissance celebrated humanity.

Into that world, Dominic, Francis, and Clare entered preaching the Gospel. Previously, those who sought to be disciples of Christ in the pursuit of "perfection," as it would be called, chose the monastery outside of any urban place. But Dominic, Francis, and Clare changed religious history by leaving the isolated monastic model to pursue the evangelization of the vibrant economic and political urban centers of Europe.

THOMAS AQUINAS

In 1224, seven years after Dominic received papal approbation for the founding of the Order of Preachers, Thomas Aquinas was born in a little town (Roccasecca, "Dry Rock" in English) in southern Italy.[8] At the age of six, Thomas's politically ambitious parents sent him to the famous Benedictine Abbey, Monte Cassino, expecting, even then, that he would eventually become abbot. The appointment would secure one of the most significant ecclesiastical titles of thirteenth-century central Italy. At fifteen, however, Thomas left the Benedictine community and, after five years of studies in Naples, he entered the relatively new order of St. Dominic.

Thomas entered the Dominicans because of their work in the towns, their promotion of the Gospel, their vow of evangelical poverty, and their newness. His family was not happy with his decision to abandon Monte Cassino for the sake of evangelical poverty. Under orders from their widowed mother, his brothers kidnapped him and held him in house detention for a year (apparently a rather frequent parental practice, considering that Francis of Assisi himself suffered the same fate). When his family relented and released him, the Dominicans made the astute decision to send Thomas away from Naples to Paris for three years of studies (1245–1248) and another four in Cologne (1248–1252). In 1252 he returned to Paris and taught his first major work, the *Commentary on the Sentences of Peter Lombard*, and then assumed the position of regent master for the Dominicans at the University of Paris. There in Paris he finished *De veritate*, began the *Summa Contra Gentiles*, and lectured on the Gospel of St. Matthew. After a brief stay in Naples (1260–1261), he went to the papal town of Orvieto for four years, where he completed the *Contra Gentiles* and his commentary on the book of Job, among other works. In 1265, he began his teaching in Rome, where he remained for three years before being summoned to return to Paris for an extraordinary second term of teaching. As we shall see, these seven years in Rome and Paris were remarkable. In 1272, he left Paris and returned to Naples for two years before he died in 1274.

Despite his girth, he was an active man. In fact, Thomas was one of history's major walkers: from Naples to Paris, Paris to Cologne, Cologne to Paris, Paris to Naples, Naples to Orvieto and then to Rome, back to Paris, and back to Naples. Not surprisingly, he collapsed while walking to the Council of Lyons. His death a few days later is ironic: the forty-nine-year-old who abandoned a vocation of Benedictine stability for the more innovative Dominican order died not in his community, but as an infirmed guest in a monastic community not far from Roccasecca and Monte Cassino.

To appreciate the specific contribution of the *Summa Theologiae*, we need to remember that four years after the founding of the Order of Preachers, Pope Innocent III gave all members in the church the requirement to confess their sins once a year just before Easter, and he specifically mandated the Dominicans to hear confessions. In response to this new apostolic charge, a few Dominicans wrote a set of confessional manuals describing sins and their gravity. These manuals became the major theological texts that most Dominicans studied. For the most part, the theological formation of Dominicans both in their early stages of life in the community as well as in their ongoing formation later in life was almost exclusively a study of the parsing of sin and its penances as found in the confessional manuals. The exception was for a few extraordinary Dominican students, like Albert, Thomas, and others, who were singled out and sent to one of the *studia*, or study centers, set up at the five major universities of Oxford, Bologna, Paris, Montpelier, and Cologne.

After being a regent master at the study center in Paris, Thomas returned to Italy and attended the provincial chapter at Anagni in the early 1260s. There he proposed an experimental study center for young Dominican students, not among the elite at the universities, but intelligent enough for something more theologically sophisticated than the confessional manuals.[9] The chapter established an experimental personal study center for Thomas at Rome, where eventually he began producing the *Summa Theologiae* for these above-average Dominican students who were open to experiments in a new order.

Thomas wrote the *Summa*, therefore, for very young men with no philosophical background but with intellectual promise. As he wrote in the preface, it was a work for "beginners." (I often think of this experiment as a forerunner of divinity schools like my own Boston College, where we train men and women fairly sophisticated academic theology for either priestly or lay ministry but not predominantly for doctoral work.)

Thomas divided the *Summa Theologiae* into three parts, with the second part having two sections. The first part is about God's relationship to us as Creator and Mover. The second part is about our response to God; the first section concerns general matters in morals, and the second treats specific virtues, vices, and sins. The third part is about Jesus Christ and the sacraments.

Thomas believed that theology should be dialogical. Nowhere is Thomas more dialogical than in this structure of the *Summa* itself. Consider the three parts: God's divine call in the first; our human response in the second; Jesus, the Word Incarnate, the indwelling of the human in the divine, and the sacraments that mediate his grace in the third. The entire work reflects a dialogue.

Each part is divided into questions and each question is divided into articles. Each article begins in the form of a question and, prior to giving an answer, we find a series of considerations from every kind of author who had ever written on the topic so as to extend the dialogue into one that includes these diverse writers. Thomas's own response to the article's question follows these considerations, and then he answers each of the points of consideration in light of his own response. Through each article Thomas invites the reader into deeper reflection, and so, before moving onto another topic, Thomas proceeds instead to another article that immediately flows from the previous answer given. These related articles become stages of a descent into the depths of inquiry first posed by the original question.

When Thomas exhausts one question, he moves on to the next. All along, the inquiring intellect of Thomas engages the reader. There are over two thousand articles in the *Summa* and through them we learn that the *Summa* is less a work of theological opinion and more a method of theological investigation.[10]

Like his work, Thomas's life was a dialogue as well. For instance, from 1269 to 1272, during his second tenure in Paris, Thomas had four scribes to whom he simultaneously (it seems) dictated—to one, the *Summa Theologiae*; to another, his commentaries on Aristotle's works (e.g., *Ethics*, *Metaphysics*, *Physics*); to another, his commentaries on the scriptures (specifically, John's Gospel and the Pauline Epistles); and to the fourth, the polemical discourses against the anti-mendicants (opponents of the newly founded Dominican and Franciscan orders) and the Averroists (the followers of Ibn Rochd [1126–1198], an Arabian philosopher who believed in the independence of philosophy from revelation).

In light of this portrait, the typical iconography of Thomas as a somewhat large but silent figure is peculiar. The man who left Monte Cassino was rarely, except in his last months, speechless. On the contrary, he was lecturing, debating, commenting, discoursing, and dictating with great relish. Moreover, one semiannual university event that he enjoyed was the Quodlibetales (in English, the "whatevers"). These sessions occurred during Advent and Lent when the entire university was assembled and random questions from the audience were submitted, dealing with whatever topic the questioner asked. While Thomas commented on the Trinity, he was also answering questions about whether one can enjoy long, warm baths.

Thomas, the man who joined the Order of Preachers, loved the Word. His theology and his life, therefore, were dialogical. His use of so many sources and his variety of interests demonstrate how convincingly he believed in the gift of human reason. No wonder, then, that he asserted that the human is made in God's image by being rational.

Through the *Summa*, then, Thomas did not only leave the reader with new insights; more important, he prompted the reader to emulate the probing intellect that wrote it. Thomas drew us into the habit of inquiring deeply.

Thomas was, of course, committed to the notion of rationality as deeply human and personal. Like other medieval Scholastics from the twelfth through the sixteenth century, Thomas investigated ways of expressing faith through reason. Inasmuch as theology was seen as a science investigating God and the human, morality specifically studied humanity as responding lovingly to the initiative of God.

This study was then highly anthropological and naturally depended on the virtues to outline an appropriate moral identity for the Christian. Virtue became then the key way that Renaissance theologians like Thomas developed their moral theology. Like everyone else in the Renaissance, Thomas was more concerned with the human being than with human action.

In the preface to the second section of the second part of the *Summa Theologiae*, Thomas wrote that all of morals comes down to the virtues. Not only did he dedicate the whole second part of the *Summa* to the virtues, but while at Paris for the second time he wrote his commentary on the *Ethics of Aristotle* (1271) as well as his works on ordinary virtues, charity, hope, and the cardinal virtues (*De virtutibus in communi*, *De caritate*, *De spe*, and *De virtutibus cardinalibus*, 1269–1272). His ethical reflection singularly revolved around the virtues.

I cannot in any adequate way summarize Thomas's work on the virtues, but I can underline certain key factors. Let me name here three. First, Thomas believed that every human action is a moral action. In order to appreciate the significance of this claim, I suggest you take an imaginary piece of paper and write down five moral matters. Did you include war, abortion, homosexuality, AIDS, racism? Probably. Probably you wrote down big issues that have great social claims on all of us. But now turn the imaginary paper over and write down five concerns with which you woke up this morning. Did those concerns include repairing a relationship; drinking less; eating less; getting more sleep; doing more work or getting more leisure; talking with your spouse, children, or boss; being less compulsive or obsessive; being less timid; being more assertive; confronting a friend; supporting a friend; being more generous? This side of the paper, I suggest, is also moral matter. Ordinary life is the matter for moral reflection, intention, and action.

When Thomas asked whether there are any actions that are free of moral meaning, he responded that if we are talking about actions in the abstract, then there are indifferent actions. Once we discuss actions that we do, however, then the only actions that are indifferent are those that we do unconsciously. He gives an example: "Stroking one's beard, unknowingly." Otherwise, everything else is about moral living. Even small actions? Yes, Thomas replies, and uses the scriptures to talk about an incidental act like breaking stalks of grain in a field.

Second, Thomas believed that we become what we do. What does this mean? Thomas appreciated that anything that we intentionally do (and he always meant intentionality in the broad sense) makes us become what we are doing. If we were rude in getting to work this morning, we are becoming ruder people. If we were able to laugh at some problems that affected us today, we are developing a sense of humor. If we stopped to help a person in need, we are growing in compassion; if we did not, we are becoming more callous.

Thomas recognized that just as we become what we do, conversely, if we only plan to act, but never realize that action, then we never realize what we can become. If I intend to speak up to my domineering boss, but never do, I will never attain the assertive stance that I believe is necessary. If I intend to give up drinking large quantities of beer, but never do, I will continue to be a heavy drinker.

Third, Thomas argued that each person ought to establish a proactive agenda. If we become what we do, then we should intend ways of acting that can shape us better into being the type of people we think we should become. Who, then, should we become? According to Thomas, we should become just, temperate, fortitudinous or steadfast, and prudent people. That is, we should acquire the cardinal virtues, which Thomas acknowledges was the position of Ambrose, Gregory, Cicero, and Augustine.

THE TRADITIONAL CARDINAL VIRTUES

The virtues are called "cardinal" from the Latin word *cardo*, which means "hinge." They are cardinal because they are "principal" in that they are fundamental hinges on which hangs our image of the moral person. Thomas wrote that these four virtues rightly order all our appetitive and intellectual powers that enable us to act: prudence orders our practical reason; justice orders the will, or our intellectual appetite; temperance and fortitude order the passions, which are divided into the concupiscible—desiring power—and the irascible—struggling power—respectively. The four virtues are cardinal because they sufficiently order all the components within us that are engaged in moral acting.[11]

In a manner of speaking, Thomas's cardinal virtues are really two. With Aristotle, Aquinas upheld the absolute priority of prudence. No cardinal virtue is more important. Prudence, of course, is not that tepid little virtue that warns us against taking bold steps. On the contrary, prudence is the virtue that looks forward to the overall end of life and sets all subsequent agendas for attaining that end and all intermediate ends. Prudence discerns and sets the standards for the pursuit of the end and therein helps us to articulate the norms of moral action. Moreover, prudence enjoys nearly the same function and authority over the moral virtues that charity does with the infused virtues: as charity unites the infused virtues, prudence unites and connects the moral virtues. In short, the "whole matter of moral virtues falls under the one rule of prudence" (*Summa Theologiae* I.II.65.1.ad3).

With what is prudence concerned? Clearly, justice. Aquinas argued that justice governs all our actions. Though the virtues of temperance and fortitude order us interiorly, justice orders all our operations or exterior actions. In a word, when we are just, we are doing things right. The virtues of temperance and fortitude are, then, auxiliaries for justice: we acquire these virtues that order our interior life for the sake of being just and doing justice. Thus, in any moral situation the prudent person asks one central question: "What is the just person to do?" In a manner of speaking, Thomas basically is asking each of us to become just people—that is, people who become, by their just actions, more and more just. [12]

PROPOSING NEW CARDINAL VIRTUES

I would like to take Thomas's cardinal virtues and suggest that for today we need to reform them somewhat. I do this reform by keeping prudence and justice and adding two other virtues that, like justice, are ends in themselves. [13] That is, I agree that temperance and fortitude are auxiliary or helping virtues and that therefore they are not really cardinal virtues.

Why do I not just let matters be? If the cardinal virtues were good enough for Cicero, Augustine, and Thomas, why can they not be sufficient for us?

I see three major reasons. First, contemporary theologians and philosophers repeatedly express dissatisfaction about the sufficiency of justice. They note that morality asks of us more than being just. For instance, my friend Marilyn Martone, a moral theologian at New York's St. John's University, reminds us that many of the twentieth century's most important advocates for justice had a variety of marital difficulties. Is not fidelity a moral virtue, and what happens when the particular obligations of marriage take one away from a more general call for justice?

For this reason, many offer hyphenated phrases, the most famous being "love-justice," which attempts to acknowledge that while working for justice—that is, the equality for all persons—we still need to maintain partial, loving relationships that must be nurtured and sustained. I find the hyphen distracting, however. We are not talking about one virtue, but in fact two distinct and sometimes opposing virtues, justice and love (or fidelity, as I and others prefer to call it). [14] For instance, many family members discover that other family members have a variety of unjust biases, but often they do not relinquish their family ties over the bias. In fact, sometimes rather than falling into perpetual dispute, one might not object to an unjust remark simply because such an objection neither improves the fidelity of the familial relationship nor diminishes the unjust bias of the family member. Or sometimes a friend might stand with another friend who is hurting after isolating him- or herself by expressing bigoted remarks. The friend recognizes the bigotry but might feel that some support is also due. Keeping alive the tension in moral theory seems then to validate the prudential recognition of the tension as it frequently arises in ordinary life.

Second, moral theologians today insist that moral dilemmas are not based on the simple opposition of good and evil but, more frequently, on the clash of goods. Thus we recognize that we cannot possibly imagine justice alone as adequate. We need a framework that raises up the possibility of other goods or cardinal virtues, like fidelity, that in the real world could conflict with one another.

Third, today we believe that the task of moral development is not for an individual to perfect her or his powers, but rather for a person to realize rightly the variety of ways that we are relational. That is, as in the way we started this discussion, we realize as they did in the twelfth century that in the image of the triune God we can only understand ourselves as relational. Therefore virtues do not realize so much interior dispositions as much as they help us to grow in the different ways that we are in relationships.

I propose, then, that the cardinal virtues are the hinges upon which depend the ways we are relational. Our identity is relational in three ways: generally, specifically, and uniquely. Each of these relational ways of being demands a cardinal virtue: as a relational being in general, we are called to justice; as a relational being specifically, we are called to fidelity; as a relational being uniquely, we are called to self-care. These three virtues are cardinal. They have equally urgent claims and they should be pursued as ends in themselves. We are not called to be faithful and self-caring in order to be just, nor are we called to be self-caring and just in order to be faithful. None is auxiliary to the others. They are cardinal. The fourth cardinal virtue is prudence, which determines what constitutes the just, faithful, and self-caring way of living, intending, and acting in the ordinary life.

Our relationality generally is directed to an ordered appreciation for the common good in which we treat all people as equal. As members of the human race, we are expected to respond to all members in general equally and impartially. That is, regardless of our familiarity with a person and regardless of our degree of attraction or repulsion to another, in justice we believe that each person is accorded the same basic fair treatment.

If justice urges us to treat all people equally, then fidelity makes very different claims. Fidelity is the virtue that nurtures and sustains the bonds of those special relationships that humans enjoy whether by blood, marriage, love, citizenship, or sacrament. If justice rests on impartiality and universality, then fidelity rests on partiality and particularity. If justice warns us against favoritism, fidelity asks us to cultivate particular relationships.

Fidelity here is like love in the "just-love" dialectic. Fidelity also addresses the claim that Carol Gilligan made in her important work, *In a Different Voice*.[15] Gilligan criticized Lawrence Kohlberg for arguing that full moral development was found in the person who could reason well about justice as impartial and universal. She countered that the human must aim both for the impartiality of justice as well as the development of particular faithful, partial bonds.

Neither of these virtues, however, addresses the unique relationship that one has with oneself. Care for self enjoys a considered role in our tradition, as, for instance, the command to love God and one's neighbor as oneself. In his writings on the order of charity, Thomas Aquinas, among others, developed this self-love at length.[16] I consider the most important task of self-care to be the formation of one's own conscience, for in that we respond to the God who calls us.

Finally, prudence has the task of integrating the three virtues into our relationships, just as it did when it was among the classical list of the cardinal virtues. Thus, prudence is always vigilantly looking to the future, trying not only to realize the claims of justice, fidelity, and self-care in the here and now, but also calling us to anticipate occasions when each of these virtues can be more fully and integratively acquired. In this way prudence is clearly a virtue that pursues ends and effectively establishes the moral agenda for the person growing in these virtues. But these ends are not really in opposition to, or in isolation from, one another. Rather, prudence helps each virtue to shape its end as more inclusive of the other two.

I also propose that all persons in every culture are constituted by these three ways of being related. I do not mean, however, that these virtues are the same everywhere. Rather the very basics or the skeleton of these virtues is present in every society. Therefore, every culture recognizes that we must respect without any partiality every person as a human being. Every culture also imposes on individuals the obligation to maintain their specific relationships to parents, children, spouse, family members, colleagues, friends, and co-citizens. A variety of loyalties call you and me to uphold the ways we are partial. Finally, every culture calls us to be responsible for our own personal well-being. Thus, wherever we are, these virtues call us to develop the three ways that each person is fundamentally relational.

Furthermore, in every culture, parents train their children in a variety of practices that help their children understand each of these virtues. Parents in New York, Nairobi, Karachi, Manila, Bogota, and Rome teach their children to respect human beings everywhere and that one should treat all persons with justice. Parents also teach their children to have a special regard for their family members. They teach them that their relatives, friends, and classmates are special and that they have particular obligations to them. Parents also teach their children to take care of themselves: to brush their teeth, to get good sleep, to study hard, to dream. Finally, parents help their children figure out ways to attain their goals. They continually mentor their children to appreciate the complexity of prudently assuming the governance of one's life. Parents patiently and consistently listen to their children to find out what they are looking for, what friendships they are wanting to develop, what projects they wish to complete, what dreams they want to realize. Parents everywhere try to help their children develop these four particular virtues: justice, fidelity, self-care, and prudence.

Though every culture proposes these three ways as necessary, every culture promotes justice, fidelity, and self-care differently. Thus these cardinal virtues do not purport to offer a picture of the ideal person, or to exhaust the entire domain of virtue. Rather than being the last word on virtue, they are the first, providing the bare essentials for right human living and specific action. As hinges, the cardinal virtues provide a skeleton of what human persons should basically be.

This skeleton gets filled out in the theater. In the very first moral drama, *Antigone*, we find the heroine perplexed over her moral dilemma. Her brothers have been involved in a great civil war and have thrown all of Thebes into chaos. They have killed one another, and the new ruler, Creon, determines that Thebans must turn away from the civil war. He rules that the unburied must remain unburied. Antigone thinks nothing of the call to impartiality. She thinks nothing of the ordinary people of Thebes. She only thinks of her brother Polyneices, who remains unburied outside the walls. She wants to be faithful to her brother even if it means Thebes will fall into civil war again and that she will be executed for burying her brother. Her sister, Ismene, arrives, thinking, well, only of herself. Her moral argument is simply "Antigone, don't do it. Our parents are dead, our brothers were fratricidal, and I only have you. If you bury him, I am without kin." The drama is riveting because it pulls us in each of the three different directions. And the reason we are so pulled is because none of the three main agents has exhibited any prudence—that is, none shows any sense of incorporating the claims of the other two virtues into their agenda.

But if you want something more contemporary and less sophisticated than *Antigone*, then see *Terminator 2*. There, a cyborg (played by Arnold Schwarzenegger) is sent to help a young boy save the world. The boy, however, is more caught up in trying to save his mother, and when forced to choose between saving seven billion humans or his mother, his sense of fidelity trumps his sense of justice. His mother, on the other hand, without any sense of self-care, insists that her son save the world. And we are sure that even after the boy saves both the world and his mother, Arnold will save the boy. Hollywood, unlike ancient Greece, never leaves us with unresolved tension.

MERCY IS WHAT MAKES THE CARDINAL VIRTUES CATHOLIC

We can say that every society enjoys these cardinal virtues but that these virtues are "thin" descriptions of the basic outline of what it means to be moral. If these virtues are "thin" when we speak of them across all the cultures of the world, then it is in specific cultures that these virtues "thicken."[17] Many philosophers and theologians, while recognizing that there are fundamental interests that all human beings share, also acknowledge the influence of local culture and therefore use this distinction between thin and thick. That is, they insist on universal though modest ways of describing basic concerns or ways of being related that are attributable to all human beings no matter where they live.[18] I am one such theologian in my "skeletal" description of how the four cardinal virtues exist in every society. I base that on the twofold premise that persons of every society are related in three fundamentally distinct ways (impartially, partially, and uniquely) and that everyone needs prudence to govern and integrate these ways.

We call these universal assertions "thin" ones, and from various cultures we seek to "thicken" them. For instance, some understanding of justice (the willingness to be impartial and to give to each her or his due) is presumably present in every culture. Justice in the United States, however, is affected considerably by the American esteem of personal autonomy and its respect of personal rights. Autonomy thickens justice inasmuch as we would not give "the due" to any persons without their consent. Our health care system, for instance, so powerfully protects the rights of the individual that we could not imagine justice in a health care system that did not privilege informed consent. This American understanding of justice differentiates itself from justice in the Philippines, where an emphasis on "smooth interpersonal relationships" governs most social relationships.

Similarly, through autonomy, American understandings of fidelity depend on the importance of mutual consent. In the Philippines, its strong emphasis on cohesion, unity, and peace clearly provides the yeast for translating fidelity into ordinary life.

Cultures give flesh to the skeletal cardinal virtues. This thickening differentiates, then, one virtue in one culture from a similar one in another. Justice, fidelity, and self-care in a Buddhist culture have somewhat similar and somewhat different meanings than they do in a liberal or Confucian context.[19]

From the beginning of this book I have argued that mercy is the trademark of Catholicism. In Catholic cultures, mercy thickens our understanding of the virtues. Inasmuch as mercy is the willingness to enter into the chaos of another so as to respond to the other, mercy thickens justice by taking into account the chaos of the most marginalized. Mercy does not temper justice, as so many believe; rather, mercy prompts us to see that justice applies to all, especially those most frequently without justice, those abandoned to the chaos of the margins. In Catholic cultures, mercy prompts justice to find the neglected, the persecuted, the oppressed, and to bring them into the solidarity of humanity by assisting them in the pursuit of their rights.

Similarly, fidelity in the many relationships we enjoy is enfleshed by mercy. Mercy helps Catholics to see from the start that no relationship is without its chaos and that every relationship requires the merciful practice of reconciliation. In Catholic marriages, for instance, the balm of mercy prompts spouses to enter one another's chaos and to forgive each other not once or twice but seventy times seven times.

Finally, the Catholic practice of self-care urges each person, through mercy, to enter into the deep chaos of one's own distinctively complicated life. By the examination of conscience we believe that the loving, merciful light of Christ illuminates every dimension of the soul and helps us to see what we need to do in the care of ourselves.

In the quest to grow as integrated, constitutively relational disciples of Christ, Catholics look to mercy to translate into practices the cardinal virtues that we all share.

STUDY QUESTIONS

1. How would you define virtue?
2. Do you think of a virtuous person as kind of nerdy? Or do you think of a virtuous person as brave, just, sensitive, articulate? Why?
3. What virtues do you most want to cultivate? Why?
4. What do you think of the new cardinal virtues?

Part III

The Task

Chapter Nine

Moral Agency

In the field of contemporary ethics today you cannot attend a conference without there being numerous papers on moral agency. It is a wonderful newly coined term that invites us to look at ourselves not simply as a people who learn moral texts and lessons, but more importantly as moral agents whose lives realize these lessons in the choices we make.

This book has been designed to highlight and promote moral agency, in particular, yours! That moral agency is so that you/we can respond from our consciences out of love to sin and suffering in the world. For that is the moral life, that is what Christ commands us in the Good Samaritan: to respond from our consciences out of love to sin and suffering. That's what the moral life comes down to, responding out of love in conscience to sin and suffering.

In this book we started with our first lesson, love, seeing that we are made in the image of God who is love. Love is where it all starts and where it all ends.

I remember sitting one night with my good friend Ken Himes on the stoop of our community. This was about three nights before I was going into extensive surgery to remove all the lymph nodes from my left leg and to see how far my stage three melanoma had traveled. I had had to wait for my surgery for one month after the biopsy, which told me that I had a malignant cancer. Waiting that month was a time of profound soul-searching. Here I was, near the eve of the surgery and I wanted to tell Ken what I had learned. I trust Ken greatly and he was going to take me to the hospital for the surgery. I said to him, "Ken, after all the searching of this month, I think it all comes down to this: the whole purpose of life is simply to love." Ken said, "Jimmy, that's what life is all about."

You don't forget conversations like that.

So when I argue that the point of departure of all moral teaching is love, I am following a truly powerful list of teachers: Jesus, Paul, John, Chrysostom, Ambrose, Augustine, Francis, Claire, Thomas, Catherine, Julian, Theresa, John of the Cross, Ignatius, Therese, Dorothy, and so on. The moral life for Catholics has always recognized the same point of departure: love, the first lesson of the moral life.

But I am also arguing from a shared life experience, an experience that has shaped my life, but that now looks to you for an assent. Can you agree with me as Ken did? Can you say, too, that that's what life is all about? Can you give me your amen?

This, above all lessons, requires your assent. If you cannot, then you can't move on.

Conscience is the second lesson. To love out of conscience is to love out of thoughtfulness.

Made in God's image we are made with the capacity to love fully and to love well. Learning to love well means aiming to respond to others according to their needs. This is a response then that demands judgment. Only out of conscience can we truly love, any other love is not worthy of our neighbor's need nor of our response.

For this reason love requires us to form our consciences, to train them, to shape them, to make them vigilant, attentive to our neighbor in need so that we do not find ourselves like the priest or the Levite on the road, passing by our neighbor in need.

It is not easy to form the conscience and for that reason the whole second half of this book is precisely about shaping the conscience.

Yahweh offered Israel the Ten Commandments precisely to shape the conscience of Israel, and those commandments today still shape Christian communities as well. From these teachings, Israel learned what it owed to God and to neighbor, understanding how the ways of God were to be the ways of Israel. The Decalogue, as the Ten Commandments have been called, gave Israel its identity and so the first of its laws was to have a singular worship for God, for Israel was God's chosen people.

These Ten Commandments govern us today and provide really the skeleton to our moral agency, framing the fundamental guidelines for moral living, shaping our consciences as we learn to love God and our neighbors as ourselves.

The Lord Jesus calls us to follow him in his footsteps, to be imitators of him because he is what we are called to be. We can remember those famous frescoes from the Sistine Chapel, where the face of Adam in the middle of the ceiling is the same face as the Risen Lord in the middle of the Last Judgment. Michelangelo understood that we are made in the image of God and therein Jesus is our beginning and our end, the alpha and the omega of all that we can possibly become.

Getting the person of Jesus right is exactly what we need to do as we begin to follow him in his footsteps. We cannot follow him unless we know him, and the better we know him, the easier it is to follow him.

Toward that end we believe that by grace we receive the virtues of faith, hope, and charity so that we can better believe and hope in the Lord and enter and maintain union with him. But Jesus also gives us the Beatitudes and, if the Ten Commandments are the alpha of scriptural teachings, then, as Lúcás Chan would say, the Beatitudes are the omega. Therein we learn that the Beatitudes teach us how by following Christ we become more like him.

Poverty of spirit leads us to a new humility where we find our place in God's world and begin to see how related we are to one another. But as we draw closer to the Lord we encounter the second beatitude, wherein we mourn for those whose lot in life is so hard. They awaken in us a solidarity that calls us to draw closer to them, to listen to them, to let their cry become our own. And as we realize that we need to respond to them, to find in ourselves the strength and the capacity and the power to change their lives, Jesus tugs at us with the third beatitude, the call to meekness that asks us to remove from our endeavors to respond the tendency to become another's redeemer. Meekness teaches us to abandon the sense of self-importance that accompanies so many champions of the poor, for it is only by meekness that we become the servants of the poor in spirit, rather than their redeeming champions.

The Beatitudes teach us how to put on Christ, and meekness places us into a very teachable moment. Not surprisingly, Jesus teaches us even more than the Beatitudes; he gives us the key to Christian living, the works of mercy right from his preaching of the parable of the King in Matthew 25. The works of mercy allow us to enter into the chaos of another, where we encounter how our neighbor looks for shelter, suffers hunger and thirst, and finds herself imprisoned. These works are the tangible ways that we train ourselves. As we respond to others.

In his *Summa Theologiae*, Thomas Aquinas asks the question: Why, if God takes away our sins through baptism, do the effects of sin remain?[1] Among the answers he gives is that these effects provide us with the opportunity for "spiritual exercises" (*spirituale exercitium*) that can help us wrestle with moral challenges within ourselves. The premier Christian spiritual exercises have been since the church's inception the works of mercy. No one can underestimate their roll in our church's life. This is why in our parishes, our schools, and our communities we teach one another to practice from a very young age the care for the sick, the hungry, the imprisoned, and the homeless. And we teach one another never to abandon this practice.

Christians are called not only to pray but to act and the training ground for learning what Christian moral agency is all about is the works of mercy. Those works make us strong. One of my favorite places on earth to visit is the very roof of the Cathedral/Duomo of Milan. On that roof you can walk all around and among other things you will see the dozens of statues of saints along the stairs and crevices throughout. When you see these saints, you cannot help but notice how athletic they look. Often, in the depictions of the saints, athleticism is conveyed, for the saints were involved in a lifetime of spiritual exercises. And the most common, basic, elemental of all spiritual exercises are the corporal works of mercy.

Thomas also teaches us that we grow in moral wisdom through the virtues and uses the word *exercises* again when he writes that virtues are gained by reflection and exercise (*studium et exercitium*). Virtues are those capacities that make us better able to live for God, ourselves, and others. Virtues literally make us strong and chief among the virtues are prudence, which teaches our conscience, and justice, which teaches us to give each what they are due. These virtues make us ready and inclined to act morally. They make us prepared for following in the footsteps of Christ.

Prudence in particular teaches us as a parent teaches a child. One of the great lessons children learn from their parents is the difference between too much and too little. They learn therein that much of life is passing between extremes. This is what good exercise is all about, no? After all, exercise is knowing not to do too little or too much. Prudence guides us in that search for just the right amount of exercise that gets us in the right place with the right amount of energy and sweat. Prudence teaches us the mean between the two extremes.

Most of the life of virtue is getting to that mean, between too much and too little. It is about getting to the just distribution of goods, the right balance of fairness, the achievement of true equity. In fact, for Thomas, what prudence most wants to get right are matters pertaining to justice.

These four texts, the Ten Commandments, the Beatitudes, the works of mercy, and the cardinal virtues, help shape our consciences to respond in love to sin and suffering.

Wherever there is conscience, there is sin. In fact, in many ways conscience is the fruit of sin. When we first recognize sin in our lives, we usually do it by feeling a certain discomfort. Our guilty consciences awaken us to something that we need to acknowledge and confess. If conscience is familiar with anything, it is sin. But that is conscience looking back at one's deeds and seeing our limits and our faults. We call the conscience that looks back to review our actions, as when we examine our consciences, a judicial conscience. A judicial conscience judges the way we act, but a legislative conscience is a forward-looking conscience that guides us on the way of the Lord.

These two perspectives, one of looking back at our past, where sin is so apparent, and the other of looking forward to the Lord who leads, provide us with a vigilance and wholeness that keeps us aware of and alert to human suffering.

The first lesson of human suffering is not to explain it away. There's just too much of human suffering. Say it again, like a mantra, "There's too much human suffering." True, we need to find the causes of suffering so that we can reduce it, but we need to be always mindful just how much suffering there is in our world. That's why Good Friday is good, because all of human suffering is, if you will, caught up in the death of Jesus: because we die, he died. He has entered so fully into our lives that his life had to end in death.

The more we realize how much suffering there is, the more we realize that we need to be always vigilant, always mindful of another in need.

Here then in these lessons and text, I hope you have learned what moral agency is about: a life that responds out of love in conscience to sin and suffering.

But before you go away, who are you?

YOU?

Who are you? Are you a single person, an individual, a lone agent? Or are you a university class or a parish group? Who are you?

The answer can start with an "I" or a "We" but in both cases, after the predictable verb, the rest of the sentence could be made up of the very same words: "I am/We are trying to understand the Christian tradition so as to live the life worthy of the call of Christian discipleship."

In many instances when we are talking about ethics we fret over whether we are addressing it to a group or an individual, but here we should see that what we say to a person, we can say to a community. Moral agency is about both.

Yet, in fact, the transition from I to we, when it comes to moral agency, is not easy.

I am writing this in the middle of one of the most horrendous immigration issues in the history of the world. Sixty million people are immigrating. One large population, fleeing Syrians, is finding itself forced into the sea, where parents have lost their children, whose lives they were protecting by their flight in the first place. I/we watch on the news and see a people pushed back from what were once open borders, forced into refugee camps. My/our own country has only added a new level of difficulty for these people to find shelter here, while our politicians are openly advocating to refuse them shelter. People here insist on calling themselves Christian, but they do not seem to hear the parable of the sheep and goats, like the part in which the goats are damned to hell with the words, "I was a stranger and you gave me no welcome" (Matt. 25:43).

I do not see what makes our country so unable to welcome others, the way, say, Canada did recently. I see instead here in my country a fear of the stranger, a lack of courage to embrace the other. But I also see a political and media machinery that capitalizes on the distrust, heightening the so-called risks that immigrants might bring. At the same time, I hear calls to monitor certain neighborhoods. I hear in all this such distrust and I see so little moral agency.

I watch the same lack of moral agency in the questions surrounding the environment. I recently took a group of university students to Managua, Nicaragua. There we visited a variety of places where people were working for development in employment, health care, education, labor, and so forth. One student asked the host of Jubilee House, where we were visiting a local health center, about the environment and whether there was any impact. The respondent let it rip about how their entire agricultural industry of coffee was radically shattered by climate change. She then said, "Only in the United States do you have the luxury to debate whether there is climate change. The rest of the world knows all too well about the effects of climate change already."[2]

These two issues highlight to me an enormous paradox. Here we live in a country of enormous power and prosperity, yet we cannot respond to the two greatest crises of our time: the environment and migration. I know how I feel, I know how friends and family around me feel, but when I look at the "we" of our society, I find such little agency, such great inertia, so little wisdom.

We could throw race into that mix. In the United States we have been unable to successfully resolve race issues. We still live in a world haunted by false assumptions, in part because, I think, we have never collectively dealt with our own social historical legacy of slavery. Slavery is our country's original sin. It is why today we cannot be reconciled over race: we never faced what we did. Our long history of slavery ends, we think, in 1865, but it never ended because we have never owned up to it. While other countries have a variety of ways of reminding themselves of their sins, trying to make sure that they never forget their histories (think for instance of the memorials to the Holocaust and other catastrophic Nazi atrocities throughout Germany), we have no national indication of our slave history. America's exceptionalism is exceptionally innocent.[3]

These instances, wherein we encounter enormous challenge yet enormous inability to respond, makes, I think, the topic of collective moral agency all the more significant.

Reinhold Niebuhr in his landmark work *Moral Man and Immoral Society*[4] explored how the individual is fundamentally unable to reconcile one's own morality with one's social context that is ethically bereft and socially immoral. More than seventy years ago Niebuhr addressed this issue and it is hard to see if there is really any advance.

I know in my life, with all its compromises, shortcomings, and sinfulness, I fall way short of the mark. But in my life I do not feel the degree of inertia, mindlessness, or banality that I do when I look at our society.

I think if you feel the way I do, then we must work more toward expanding the range and depth of the "we" that constitutes "us." I think the lessons that you found in this book, whether you found them alone or with a group, need to be shared all the more urgently.

I think that we cannot leave our society alone. I think in our society there is a lot wrong, a lot of sin, but also a lot of suffering. We need to address that reality as well as the challenges of immigration, race, and environment. We are called to a new awareness of waking one another up to a new kenotic moment, a new defining time. Unless we become more than ourselves, then this world of ours, already overcome by fear, will only continue sliding away. It strikes me that now, the question of moral agency in this country is the most critical moral question.

Just last week I was interviewed on the radio and I remarked how striking it was for me as a seven-year-old to hear President Kennedy say, "Ask not what your country can do for you, ask what you can do for your country." The interviewer, reading my thoughts, said: "So few hear that challenge today. They hear instead, I ask what my country can do for me." I think that the "American We" needs to reawaken itself to these moral lessons and we Catholics need to share all the more our lessons and texts—no, not to proselytize, but to learn again and again that the call to love is the call to answer the need of one's neighbor wherever they are.

Consider again the parable of the Good Samaritan. In that one parable we learn who the neighbor is, that mercy constitutes entering the chaos of another, that the call to love is a call to respond actively to the one in need, but that all these lessons are made possible first by the deeds of the merciful Christ, who has been our own personal Good Samaritan. That is, Christ's actions make possible in us our healing so that we can attend to others.

Because Christ's actions have been continuous for two millennia and because the church has been that inn where we have all been brought to live, we have learned that we can only respond to our neighbor in need because we were first recognized by Christ as in need ourselves. We know within ourselves what Christ has already accomplished in us.

What Christ has accomplished in us is not something that remains in ideas or dreams or wishes. What he has won for us are timeless lessons for living and loving. We need to share them and not just keep them as our own.

Notes

INTRODUCTION

1. John Mahoney, *The Making of Moral Theology: A Study of the Roman Catholic Tradition* (New York: Oxford University Press, 1987).

2. James F. Keenan, "John Mahoney's *The Making of Moral Theology*" in Gilbert Meilaender and William Werpehowski, eds., *Oxford Handbook of Theological Ethics* (Oxford: Oxford University Press, 2005), 503–19.

3. John T. McNeill and Helen M. Gamer, eds., *Medieval Handbooks of Penance* (New York: Columbia University Press, 1990).

4. Henry Lea, *The History of Auricular Confession and Indulgences in the Latin Church* (Philadelphia: Lea Brothers, 1896), 1.230.

5. Leonard Boyle, *The Setting of the* Summa Theologiae *of Saint Thomas* (Toronto: Pontifical Institute of Medieval Studies, 1982).

6. Thomas Slater, *A Manual of Moral Theology*, 2nd ed. (New York: Benziger Brothers, 1908), vol. 1, 5–6. In his "Cases of Conscience," he writes that the object of moral theology "is not to place high ideals of virtue before the people and train them in Christian perfection . . . its primary object is to teach the priest how to distinguish what is sinful from what is lawful . . . it is not intended for edification nor for the building up of character." As quoted in Henry McAdoo, *The Structure of Caroline Moral Theology* (London: Longmans, 1949), 10–11.

7. Second Vatican Council, "Optatam Totius," http://www.vatican.va/archive/hist_councils/ii_vatican_council/documents/vat-ii_decree_19651028_optatam-totius_en.html.

8. Margaret Farley, "How Shall We Love in a Postmodern World?" in *The Annual of the Society of Christian Ethics 1994*, ed. Harlan Beckley (Washington, DC: Georgetown University Press, 1994), 3–10.

1. LOVE

1. Josef Fuchs, *Human Values and Christian Morality* (Dublin: Gill and MacMillan, 1970).

2. Pope John Paul II, "The Splendor of the Truth," *Origins*, October 14, 1993, 297–336; Joseph Cardinal Ratzinger, *Wahrheit, Werte, Macht: Prüfsteine der pluralistischen Gesellschaft* (Freiburg, Germany: Herder, 1993).

3. Benedict XVI, *Deus Caritas Est*, http://w2.vatican.va/content/benedict-xvi/en/encyclicals/documents/hf_ben-xvi_enc_20051225_deus-caritas-est.html.

4. James Keenan, *Commandments of Compassion* (Franklin, WI: Sheed & Ward, 1999).

5. Karl Rahner, *Foundations of Christian Faith: An Introduction to the Idea of Christianity* (New York: Herder and Herder, 1983).

6. Gérard Gilleman, *The Primacy of Charity in Moral Theology* (Westminster, MD: Newman Press, 1959). See also Peter Black and James Keenan, "The Evolving Self-Understanding of the Moral Theologian: 1900–2000," *Studia Moralia* 39 (2001): 291–327.

7. St. Augustine, *The Confessions of St. Augustine*, book 10, paragraph 27.

8. Edward Vacek, *Love, Human and Divine: The Heart of Christian Ethics* (Washington, DC: Georgetown University Press, 1994); Vacek, "Love for God—Is It Obligatory?" in *The Annual of the Society of Christian Ethics 1996*, ed. Harlan Beckley (Washington, DC: Georgetown University Press, 1996), 203–22; Vacek, "The Eclipse of Love for God," *America*, March 9, 1996, 13–16.

9. Margaret Farley, *Personal Commitments* (San Francisco: Harper & Row, 1986), 131–32; Farley, "New Patterns of Relationship between Women and Men: The Beginnings of a Moral Revolution," *Theological Studies* 36 (1975): 627–46; Farley, "How Shall We Love in a Postmodern World?" in *The Annual of the Society of Christian Ethics 1994*, ed. Harlan Beckley (Washington, DC: Georgetown University Press, 1994), 3–10.

10. Frederick Crowe, "Complacency and Concern in the Thought of St. Thomas," *Theological Studies* 20 (1959): 1–39, 198–230, 343–95.

11. Hugo Rahner, *Ignatius the Theologian* (New York: Herder and Herder, 1968).

12. Stephen Pope, *The Evolution of Altruism and the Ordering of Love* (Washington, DC: Georgetown University Press, 1994); see also his "Expressive Individualism and True Self-Love: A Thomistic Perspective," *Journal of Religion* 71, no. 3 (1991): 384–99.

2. CONSCIENCE

1. "In hoc quippe mundo humana anima quasi more navis est contra ictum fluminis conscendentis: uno in loco nequaquam stare permittitur, quia ad ima relabitur, nisi ad summa conetur." Gregory, *Reg. Past.* p. III, c. 34: ML 77, 118c.

2. "In via vitae non progredi regredi est." Bernard, *Serm* II in festo. Purif., n. 3: ML 183, 369c.

3. "In via Dei stare retrocedere est." Thomas attributes the quote to Bernard in *In III Sen* d29, a8, qla2, 1a, and to Gregory in ST II-II.24.6, ob3.

4. Paul VI, *Gaudium et Spes* (1965), http://www.vatican.va/archive/hist_councils/ii_vatican_council/documents/vat-ii_const_19651207_gaudium-et-spes_en.html.

5. John Glaser, "Conscience and Superego: A Key Distinction," *Theological Studies* 32 (1971): 30–47, at 36.

6. Thomas Aquinas, *Scriptum super libros Sententiarum*, IV. 38.2.4, q.a. 3; see also IV.27.1.2., q.a. 4, ad3; IV.27.3.3, expositio. Besides his *Commentary*, Thomas established clearly in *De veritate* (q. 17, a. 4.), the Quodlibetales (III.12.27; VIII.6.13; IX.7), his commentaries on Romans (chap. 14, lect. 2), and Galatians (5, lect. 1) and the *Summa Theologiae* (I.II, q. 19, a. 5) that it is always sinful to go against one's conscience.

7. James F. Keenan, "Can a Wrong Action Be Good? The Development of Theological Opinion on Erroneous Conscience," *Église et Théologie* 24 (1993): 205–21.

8. On this distinction, see James F. Keenan, "A New Distinction in Moral Theology: Being Good and Living Rightly," *Church* 5 (1989): 22–28; and Keenan, *Goodness and Rightness in Thomas Aquinas' Summa Theologiae* (Washington, DC: Georgetown University Press, 1992).

9. Francis Connell, *Outlines of Moral Theology* (Milwaukee, WI: Bruce Publishing Company, 1953), 39.

10. Iris Murdoch, "Against Dryness: A Polemical Sketch," in *Revisions*, ed. Stanley Hauerwas and Alasdair MacIntyre (Notre Dame, IN: University of Notre Dame Press, 1983), 43–50, at 43.

11. For more on conscience, see my "Redeeming Conscience," *Theological Studies* 76, no. 1 (May 2015): 129–47.

3. SIN

1. I should note that invariably those with poor self-esteem and other truly burdensome dispositions read this and are not helped. They think I am suggesting that they should think worse of themselves. But I am not. It helps us to remember the old saying that virtue is the mean between extremes. Thus, courage is the mean between cowardice and foolhardiness. Similarly, we have a tendency to over- and underestimate ourselves. Those with low self-esteem underestimate themselves. My warning is for those of us (myself included) who overestimate themselves.

2. James F. Keenan, "The Problem with Thomas Aquinas's Concept of Sin," *Heythrop Journal* 35 (1994): 401–20.

3. John Mahoney, *The Making of Moral Theology* (Oxford: Clarendon Press, 1987), 32.

4. Albert Camus, *The Plague* (New York: Vintage Press, 1991).

5. David Burrell and Stanley Hauerwas, "Self-Deception and Autobiography," in *Truthfulness and Tragedy*, by Stanley Hauerwas, Richard Bondi, and David B. Burrell (Notre Dame, IN: University of Notre Dame Press, 1977), 82–100.

6. Franz Böckle, *Fundamental Moral Theology* (New York: Pueblo Publishing, 1980).

7. I do not mean by the failure to bother to love the example of being angry with someone. That may or may not be out of love. The issue in these chapters on sin and conscience is not how we love rightly, a very big issue indeed, but rather whether we love in the first place.

8. Martin Luther King Jr., "Letter from Birmingham City Jail," in *A Testament of Hope: The Essential Writings of Martin Luther King, Jr.*, ed. James M. Washington (San Francisco: Harper and Row, 1986), 289–302; Reinhold Niebuhr, *Moral Man and Immoral Society: A Study in Ethics and Politics* (New York: Scribner, 1960).

9. On the different understandings of this parable, see Gilbert Meilaender, "Grace, Justification through Faith, and Sin," in *Ecumenical Ventures in Ethics: Protestants Engage Pope John Paul II's Moral Encyclicals*, ed. Reinhard Hutter and Theodor Dieter (Grand Rapids, MI: Eerdmans, 1997), 60–83.

10. For more recent writings on sin, see my "Raising Expectations on Sin," *Theological Studies* 77, no. 1 (March 2016): 165–80.

4. SUFFERING

1. Daniel Simundson, *Faith Under Fire* (Minneapolis: Augsburg Publishing, 1980), 144.

2. Elaine Scarry, *The Body in Pain: The Making and Unmaking of the World* (New York: Oxford University, 1985), 27–59, at 49.

3. J. David Pleins, "'Why Do You Hide Your Face?' Divine Silence and Speech in the Book of Job," *Interpretation* 48 (July 1994): 229–40, at 230.

4. Marcel Sarot, "Auschwitz, Morality and the Suffering of God," *Modern Theology* 7 (1991): 135–52.

5. Paul Nelson, "The Problem of Suffering," *The Christian Century* 108 (May 1, 1991): 491.

6. Barbara Bozak, "Suffering and the Psalms of Lament," *Église et Théologie* 23 (1992): 325–38.

7. M. Shawn Copeland, "'Wading Through Many Sorrows': Towards a Theology of Suffering in a Womanist Perspective," in *Feminist Ethics and the Catholic Moral Tradition*, ed. Charles Curran, Margaret Farley, and Richard McCormick (New York: Paulist Press, 1996), 150.

8. Ibid., 152–53.

9. Ibid., 156.

10. Eric Cassell, *The Nature of Suffering* (New York: Oxford University Press, 1991), 24–25.

11. Ibid., 31.

12. Edward Schillebeeckx, *Christ* (New York: Seabury Press, 1980), 675.

13. Ibid., 677.

14. Ibid., 678.

15. Ibid., 724–25.

16. Ibid., 728.

17. William Placher, *Narratives of a Vulnerable God* (Louisville, KY: Westminster, 1994), 18–19.

18. Mary Catherine Hilkert, *Speaking with Authority* (New York: Paulist Press, 2001), 126.

19. Judith M. Noone, *The Same Fate as the Poor* (Maryknoll, NY: Orbis, 1995), 82, quoted in Hilkert, *Speaking with Authority*, 127.

20. Sheila Cassidy, *Good Friday People* (Maryknoll, NY: Orbis, 1991), 61, quoted in Hilkert, *Speaking with Authority*, 128.

5. THE TEN COMMANDMENTS

1. Francisco de Toledo, *Summa Casuum Conscientiae Sive De Instructione Sacerdotum, Libri Septem* (Constantiae: Apud Nicolaum Kalt, 1600).

2. I have developed this in "The Casuistry of Francisco de Toledo (1532–1596)," *Mercurian Collection*, ed. Thomas McCoog (St. Louis, MO: St. Louis University Press, 2003).

3. Feliciano Cereceda, "Tolet, François," in *Dictionnaire de théologie catholique*, ed. Bernard Loth and Albert Michel (Paris: Letouzey et Ané, 1953–1972), 15:1223–25.

4. Toledo, *Summa Casuum Conscientiae*, fol. 463.

5. Ibid., fol. 344.

6. Ibid., fol. 428.

7. Yiu Sing Lúcás Chan, *The Ten Commandments and the Beatitudes: Biblical Studies and Ethics for Real Life* (Lanham, MD: Rowman & Littlefield, 2012), 141–42. See Raymond E. Brown, *An Introduction to the New Testament* (New York: Doubleday, 1997), 178.

8. Pope John Paul II, *Veritatis Splendor*, August 6, 1993, para. 12–16, http://w2.vatican.va/content/john-paul-ii/en/encyclicals/documents/hf_jp-ii_enc_06081993_veritatis-splendor.html.

9. Pontifical Biblical Commission, *The Bible and Morality: Biblical Roots of Christian Conduct*, 2008, http://www.vatican.va/roman_curia/congregations/cfaith/pcb_documents/rc_con_cfaith_doc_20080511_bibbia-e-morale_en.html.

10. Lúcás Chan, S.J., *Biblical Ethics in the 21st Century: Developments, Emerging Consensus, and Future Directions* (Mahwah, NJ: Paulist Press, 2013).

11. Chan, "A Hermeneutical Proposal," *Biblical Ethics in the 21st Century*, 78–112.

12. Chan, *The Ten Commandments*, 63–72.

13. Louis Vereecke, *Storia del riposo domenicale* (Rome: Alfonsianum Press, 1973).

14. Bryan Massingale, "The African American Experience and U.S. Roman Catholic Ethics: 'Strangers and Aliens No Longer'?" in *Black and Catholic: The Challenge and Gift of Black Folk: Contributions of African American Experience and World View to Catholic Theology*, ed. Jamie Phelps (Milwaukee, WI: Marquette University Press, 1997).

15. Chan, *The Ten Commandments*, 73–81.

16. Ibid., 233. See Confucius, *Confucian Analects, the Great Learning and the Doctrine of the Mean*, trans. James Legge (New York: Dover Publications, 1971).

17. Chan, *The Ten Commandments*, 83.

18. Ibid., 83–92.

6. JESUS IN THE NEW TESTAMENT

1. Stanley Hauerwas, *A Community of Character* (Notre Dame, IN: University of Notre Dame Press, 1981).

2. John Paul II, *Veritatis Splendor*, sec. 16, http://w2.vatican.va/content/john-paul-ii/en/encyclicals/documents/hf_jp-ii_enc_06081993_veritatis-splendor.html.

3. Ibid., 16.

4. Yiu Sing Lúcás Chan, *The Ten Commandments and the Beatitudes: Biblical Studies and Ethics for Real Life* (Lanham, MD: Rowman & Littlefield, 2012), 162.

5. Ibid, 164.

6. Ibid., 171.

7. Ibid.

8. Ibid.

9. Ibid., 172.

10. Ibid., 173.

11. Ibid., 178.

12. Ibid., 180.

13. Ibid., 181. From Monika K. Hellwig, "The Blessedness of the Meek, the Merciful, and the Peacemakers," in *New Perspectives on the Beatitudes*, ed. Francis A. Eigo (Villanova, PA: The Villanova University Press, 1995), 193.

14. James Gustafson, *Theology and Christian Ethics* (Philadelphia: United Church Press, 1974), 121–45; see also Richard Gula, *Reason Informed by Faith: Foundations of Catholic Morality* (New York: Paulist Press, 1989), 165–84.

7. PRACTICING THE CORPORAL WORKS OF MERCY

1. William Spohn, *Go and Do Likewise: Jesus and Ethics* (New York: Continuum Press, 1999).

2. Rodney Stark, *The Rise of Christianity* (Princeton, NJ: Princeton University Press, 1996), 147.

3. Ibid., 212.

4. This information is culled from a variety of sources, especially Théodore Koehler, "Miséricorde," in *Dictionnaire de spiritualité ascétique et mystique, doctrine et histoire*, ed. Marcel Viller (Paris: G. Beauchesne et ses fils, 1980), 10:1313–28; Írenée Noye, "Miséricorde (Oeuvres de)," in *Dictionnaire*, 10:1328–50; J. M. Perrin, "Mercy, Works of," in *New Catholic Encyclopedia* (Washington, DC: Catholic University of America Press, 1967), 676–78.

5. John O'Malley, *The First Jesuits* (Cambridge, MA: Harvard University Press, 1993), 167–78.

6. Sr. Helen Prejean, *Dead Man Walking: An Eyewitness Account of the Death Penalty in the United States* (New York: Vintage Press, 1994).

7. For more on the practice of mercy, see my *The Works of Mercy: The Heart of Catholicism* (Lanham, MD: Sheed & Ward, 2007).

8. CULTIVATING THE CARDINAL VIRTUES

1. Joseph de Guibert, *The Theology of the Spiritual Life* (New York: Sheed & Ward, 1953); Jean Leclercq, Francois Vandenbroucke, and Louis Bouyer, *History of Christian Spirituality* (London: Burns and Oates, 1968).

2. Bernard McGinn, "The Human Person as Image of God," in *Christian Spirituality*, ed. Jean Leclercq, Bernard McGinn, and John Meyendorff (New York: Crossroad, 1985), 312–30, at 323. While the twelfth century marks the enormous systematic development of ascetical texts, a few appear earlier, for example, Dhuoda's *Manual for My Son* (843) and Jonas of Orleans's treatise *Instruction of the Laity* (ca. 828). See Jacques Fontaine, "The Practice of Christian Life: The Birth of the Laity," in *Christian Spirituality*, 453–91.

3. Caroline Walker Bynum, *Jesus as Mother: Studies in the Spirituality of the High Middle Ages* (Berkeley: University of California Press, 1982), 109.

4. Ibid., 86.

5. Francois Vandenbroucke, "Lay Spirituality in the Twelfth Century," in *History of Christian Spirituality*, 243–82.

6. Bynum, *Jesus as Mother*, 106.

7. Ibid., 106.

8. On Thomas's life, the finest work is James Weisheipl, *Friar Thomas d'Aquino*, 2nd ed. (Washington, DC: Catholic University of America Press, 1983). The best work on his writing is Jean-Pierre Torrell, *Saint Thomas Aquinas* (Washington, DC: Catholic University of America Press, 1996).

9. Leonard Boyle, *The Setting for the* Summa Theologiae (Toronto: Pontifical Institute of Medieval Studies, 1982).

10. The best introduction to Thomas Aquinas's very different methods remains Marie Dominique Chenu, *Toward Understanding Saint Thomas* (Chicago: Henry Regnery, 1963).

11. See Josef Pieper, *The Four Cardinal Virtues* (Notre Dame, IN: University of Notre Dame Press, 1966); Jean Porter, *The Recovery of Virtue* (Louisville, KY: Westminster, 1990).

12. For an excellent companion to reading the second part of the *Summa Theologiae*, see Stephen Pope, ed., *The Ethics of Aquinas* (Washington, DC: Georgetown University Press, 2002).

13. I develop this in "Proposing Cardinal Virtues," *Theological Studies* 56 (1995): 709–29.

14. Paul Ricoeur, "Love and Justice," in *Radical Pluralism and Truth: David Tracy and the Hermeneutics of Religion*, ed. Werner G. Jeanrond and Jennifer L. Rike (New York: Crossroad, 1991), 187–202, at 196.

15. Carol Gilligan, *In a Different Voice: Psychological Theory and Women's Development* (Cambridge, MA: Harvard University Press, 1982).

16. Stephen Pope, "Expressive Individualism and True Self-Love: A Thomistic Perspective," *Journal of Religion* 71, no. 3 (1991): 384–99; Edward Collins Vacek, *Love, Human and Divine* (Washington, DC: Georgetown University Press, 1994), 239–73.

17. I develop this in "Virtue and Identity," in *Creating Identity: Biographical, Moral, Religious*, ed. Hermann Häring, Maureen Junker-Kenny, and Dietmar Mieth (London: SCM Press, 2000), 69–77.

18. For example, Martha Nussbaum, "Non-Relative Virtues: An Aristotelian Approach," in *Ethical Theory: Character and Virtue*, ed. Peter A. French, Theodore E. Uehling Jr., and Howard K. Wettstein, Midwest Studies in Philosophy, vol. 13 (Notre Dame, IN: University of Notre Dame Press, 1988), 32–53.

19. Lee H. Yearley, *Mencius and Aquinas: Theories of Virtue and Conceptions of Courage* (Albany: State University of New York Press, 1990).

9. MORAL AGENCY

1. Thomas Aquinas, *Summa Theologiae*, III.69.3c, http://www.newadvent.org/summa/4069.htm#article3.

2. An organization that I helped found, Catholic Theological Ethics in the World Church (http://www.catholicethics.com), has dedicated itself to several of these issues. See Christiana Z. Peppard and Andrea Vicini, eds., *Just Sustainability: Technology, Ecology, and Resource Extraction* (Maryknoll, NY: Orbis Books, 2015); Agnes Brazal and M. T. Davila, *Catholic*

Theological Ethics on the Migrations of Peoples: Living with(out) Borders (Maryknoll, NY: Orbis Books, 2016).

3. M. Shawn Copeland, *Enfleshing Freedom: Body, Race, and Being* (Minneapolis: Fortress Press, 2010); Bryan N. Massingale, *Racial Justice and the Catholic Church* (Maryknoll, NY: Orbis Books, 2010); James F. Keenan, "Raising Expectations on Sin," *Theological Studies* 77, no. 1 (March 2016): 165–80.

4. Reinhold Niebuhr, *Moral Man and Immoral Society: A Study in Ethics and Politics* (Philadelphia: Westminster/John Knox Press, 2013).

Index

About the Author

Fr. James F. Keenan, S.J., is the Canisius Professor, director of the Jesuit Institute, and director of the Gabelli Presidential Scholars Program at Boston College. A Jesuit priest since 1982, he received a licentiate (1984) and a doctorate (1988) from the Pontifical Gregorian University in Rome.

He has edited or written nineteen books and published more than three hundred essays, articles, and reviews in more than twenty-five international journals. He has been a fellow at the Institute of Advanced Studies at the University of Edinburgh (1994), the Center of Theological Inquiry, Princeton (1995, 1996), and the Instituto Trentino di Cultura (2007, 2008). He has been adjunct professor at the Gregorian University in Rome (2000, 2002), Loyola School of Theology in Manila (2001, 2003, 2004), Dharmaram Vidya Kshetram in Bangalore (2007, 2009, 2012, 2015), and Jnana-Deepa Vidyapeeth in Pune, India (2015). He held the Tuohy Chair at John Carroll University, Cleveland (1999), and the Gasson Chair at Boston College (2003–2005).

He is the founder of Catholic Theological Ethics in the World Church (CTEWC) and chaired the First International Cross-Cultural Conference for Catholic Theological Ethicists in July 2006 in Padua, Italy. He subsequently edited the conference papers that appeared as *Catholic Theological Ethics in the World Church: The Plenary Papers from the First Cross-Cultural Conference on Catholic Theological Ethics* with publishing houses in New York, Buenos Aires, Bologna, Bangalore, São Paolo, and Manila. In 2010, he hosted another international conference of theological ethicists in Trento, Italy, and published those papers in New York, Bangalore, Manila, and Buenos Aires as *Catholic Theological Ethics, Past, Present, and Future: The Trento Conference*. Today CTEWC is a live network of more than one thousand Catholic ethicists (http://www.catholicethics.com).

From 1994 to 2013, he was the series editor of Moral Traditions at Georgetown University Press and published fifty-two books. Among his own recent books are *A History of Catholic Moral Theology in the Twentieth Century: From Confessing Sins to Liberating Consciences* (2010); *Ethics of the Word: Voices in the Catholic Church Today* (Rowman & Littlefield, 2010); and, with Dan Harrington, *Paul and Virtue Ethics* (Rowman & Little-field, 2010). He recently authored *University Ethics: How Colleges Can Build and Benefit from a Culture of Ethics* (Rowman & Littlefield, 2015) and edited, with Yiu Sing Lúcás Chan and Shaji George Kochuthara, *Doing Catholic Theological Ethics in a Cross-Cultural and Interreligious Asian Context* (2016). He is presently writing *A Brief History of Catholic Ethics* and has finished editing, with Yiu Sing Lúcás Chan and Ronaldo Zacharias, *The Bible and Catholic Theological Ethics*.

He is planning for the next conference of CTEWC to be held in July 2018 in Sarajevo.

CPSIA information can be obtained
at www.ICGtesting.com
Printed in the USA
BVHW070205231021
619501BV00003B/7